YOU ARE HERE

ALSO BY ADA LIMÓN

YOU ARE HERE

POETRY IN THE

NATURAL WORLD

Edited and introduced by

ADA LIMÓN

24TH POET LAUREATE OF THE UNITED STATES

Published by MILKWEED EDITIONS,
in association with THE LIBRARY OF CONGRESS

 milkweed EDITIONS

Published 2024 by Milkweed Editions
Printed in Canada
Cover design by Mary Austin Speaker
Cover art by Enikö Katalin Eged
Author photo by Lucas Marquardt
24 25 26 27 28   5 4 3 2 1
First Edition

Library of Congress Cataloging-in-Publication Data

Names: Limón, Ada, editor.
Title: You are here : poetry in the natural world / edited and introduced
by Ada Limón, 24th Poet Laureate of the United States.
Description: First edition. | Minneapolis, Minnesota : Milkweed Editions,
in association with the Library of Congress, 2024. | Includes index. |
Summary: "Published in association with the Library of Congress and
edited by the twenty-fourth Poet Laureate of the United States, a
singular collection of fifty poems reflecting on our relationship to the
natural world by our most celebrated writers"-- Provided by publisher.
Identifiers: LCCN 2023052612 (print) | LCCN 2023052613 (ebook) | ISBN
9781571315687 (hardcover) | ISBN 9781571317926 (ebook)
Subjects: LCSH: American poetry--21st century. | Nature--Poetry. | LCGFT:
Poetry.
Classification: LCC PS595.N22 Y68 2024 (print) | LCC PS595.N22 (ebook) |
DDC 811/.608036--dc23/eng/20231109
LC record available at https://lccn.loc.gov/2023052612
LC ebook record available at https://lccn.loc.gov/2023052613

Milkweed Editions is committed to ecological stewardship. We strive to align our book
production practices with this principle, and to reduce the impact of our operations in
the environment. We are a member of the Green Press Initiative, a nonprofit coalition
of publishers, manufacturers, and authors working to protect the world's endangered
forests and conserve natural resources. *You Are Here* was printed on acid-free 100%
postconsumer-waste paper by Friesens Corporation.

Contents

"The land is the real teacher."

—ROBIN WALL KIMMERER

YOU
ARE
HERE

Foreword

As part of her signature project, "You Are Here," 24th US Poet Laureate Ada Limón has commissioned fifty-two contemporary American poets to observe and reflect on their place in the natural world. The resulting anthology of original poems is a timely portrait of the myriad ways the natural world speaks to us and reflects us. Some of the poems included here contend with the destruction of nature, while others consider its abundance and resilience—and some do both at the same time. While these poems emerge from deeply personal perspectives, together they reveal that nature, like poetry, is universal—and that our interpretations of the natural world are grounded in the nature of our humanity. They also serve as a call for readers to take in the nature all around them, wherever they are.

This anthology goes hand in hand with Limón's other project initiative, "You Are Here: Poetry in Parks," which brings poetry installations to seven national parks across the country. These installations, which transform picnic tables into works of public art, each feature a historic American poem that connects in a meaningful way to the park—helping visitors experience anew some of the country's most iconic landscapes.

Limón's passionate championship of poetry—she wrote a poem for the National Climate Assessment and even partnered with NASA to send a poem into space—aligns beautifully with the Library of Congress's long history of supporting poetry through its public programs and initiatives and through its collections. I invite you to explore the Library's many holdings related to poetry in person or online at loc.gov.

CARLA HAYDEN,
Librarian of Congress

Introduction

There's a tree I planted at the edge of the yard on my birthday a few years ago: a small Jane magnolia bred for beauty and pleasure, and it has given me both. I'm staring at that tree now as the wind is coming up and the weather is turning from sun-bright to cloud-covered quickly, dramatically. It's no secret that when I am trying to find myself, trying to ground myself, I stare at trees. I first see them as a green blur of soothing movement, something distant trembling in unison, but then I look at the leaves, remembering the names.

From where I sit now, I can see the magnolia, the three cypress trees, the hackberry, and the old mulberry tree that drapes its tired branches over everything like it wants to give up but won't. Watching them makes me feel at once more human and less human. I become aware that I am in a body, yes, but it is a body connected to these trees, and we are breathing together.

You might not know this, but poems are like trees in this way. They let us breathe together. In each line break, caesura, and stanza, there's a place for us to breathe. Not unlike a redwood forest or a line of crepe myrtles in an otherwise cement landscape, poems can be a place to stop and remember that we too are living. W.S. Merwin wrote in his poem "Place": "On the last day of the world, I would want to plant a tree." I think I would add that I would also like to write a poem. Maybe I'd even write a poem about a tree?

When I was first asked what I wanted to create for a national poetry project during my tenure as the 24th Poet Laureate of the United States, I remember staring out the window of my office in the Library of Congress thinking, I just want us all to write poems and save the planet. I might have even said just that. And of course, that seemed impossible. A poem can seem so small, so minor, so invisible, especially when up against the daily crises and catastrophes that our planet is facing. And that's not to mention the hardships that we each face both publicly and privately. How can a poem make a difference? How can a tree make a difference?

Perhaps the answer to those questions is that poetry and nature have a way of simply reminding us that we are not alone. The Kentucky writer bell hooks once wrote, "Rarely, if ever, are any of us healed in isolation. Healing is an act of communion." Going to the woods, or simply noticing the small defiant ways nature is thriving all around me on a daily basis, helps me feel that communion. And poems, like the poems that I've collected here for this anthology, help me feel that sense of communion too.

When creating green spaces or attempting to rewild an area, it's not about planting one tree, but many. It's not simply about the overstory, but the wild grasses and shrubs and living creatures in the understory. This anthology hopes to be both the canopy and the soil— not just a community, but a living ecosystem made stronger by all its parts. As Robin Wall Kimmerer wrote in *Braiding Sweetgrass*, "All flourishing is mutual."

A short while ago I was walking on a trail near where I live in Kentucky, and before I set off for my hike, I studied the map to determine if I wanted to go to the falls or the rocky outcropping that is the river overlook. My brain that day was full of bad news. The climate crisis was presenting itself in furious and disastrous ways all over the globe, the human element was behaving no less ruthlessly. My anxiety was rising and I could feel my heart beating loudly against the walls of my chest. *How do we live?* That was the question that kept returning to my mind. How do we live?

As I stared at the trail map, I saw the friendly little red arrow that pointed to where I was on the map, its caption: You Are Here. It seemed not only to serve as a locator, but as a reminder that I was living right now, breathing in the woods, that there was life around me, that the natural world was right here and I was a part of it; I was nature too.

That day, I walked the waterfalls, where water runs clear and cold through the soft hills. I was totally alone and each time my brain wanted to reach toward something awful—I was reminded that I was here. I repeated, *you are here, you are here.* And *you* are too. We are here, together in this moment, crucial and urgent, yes, but also full of wonder and awe at every turn.

You Are Here: Poetry in the Natural World is an offering, something manifested out of care and attention, but also need. In these pages there are poems dedicated to our ancestors, like the poems from Rigoberto González and Carolyn Forché that bear witness to our past, and poems to our children and grandchildren, like the poems from Matthew Zapruder and Ellen Bass that worry for our future. Most of all, these poems honor what feelings and lessons nature gives us. In her poem, Dorianne Laux writes, "I felt large inside my life," and Victoria Chang writes in hers, "In Alaska, my life was with me again, attached for now." Patricia Smith allows for a vibrating instruction in her poem: "Blossom when you're ready, but rough." Here, poems serve as a witnessing as much as they do incantations.

If in order to have one tree flourish, we must plant more around it, the same must go for poems. The words collected here—in this small forest of poetry—were made specifically for this anthology, and they are some of the finest I have ever read. From rhapsodic love poems about natural landscapes and vibrant odes to trees and sky to poems that ache with what we have lost and fear for what we might become, these poems represent the full spectrum of how we human animals connect to the natural world.

I hope you will consider making your own version of a "You Are Here" poem to grow alongside ours—whether you put pen to paper or visit a beloved national park or plant potted flowers on your stoop in Brooklyn—so we may continue to flourish. I hope this anthology serves as a reminder that there is more time to plant trees, to write poems, to not just be in wonder at this planet, but to offer something back to it, to offer something back together.

Because nature is not a place to visit. Nature is who we are.

ADA LIMÓN,
24th Poet Laureate of the United States

Carrie Fountain

Carrie Fountain is a poet, novelist, and children's book author. She is the author of three poetry collections—*The Life, Instant Winner,* and *Burn Lake,* which won the National Poetry Series Award—and the novel *I'm Not Missing.* Her children's book, *The Poem Forest,* tells the story of American poet W.S. Merwin and the palm forest he grew from scratch on the island of Maui. Her poems have appeared in *Poetry,* the *American Poetry Review,* and the *New Yorker,* among many other publications. In 2019, Fountain was named Poet Laureate of Texas, where she currently lives.

YOU BELONG TO THE WORLD

as do your children, as does your husband.
It's strange even now to understand that
you are a mother and a wife, that these gifts
were given to you and that you received them,
fond as you've always been of declining
invitations. You belong to the world. The hands
that put a peach tree into the earth exactly
where the last one died in the freeze belong
to the world and will someday feed it again,
differently, your body will become food again
for something, just as it did so humorously
when you became a mother, hungry beings
clamoring at your breast, born as they'd been
with the bodily passion for survival that is
our kind's one common feature. You belong
to the world, animal. Deal with it. Even as
the great abstractions come to take you away,
the regrets, the distractions, you can at any second
come back to the world to which you belong,
the world you never left, won't ever leave, cells
forever, forever going through their changes,
as they have been since you were less than
anything, simple information born inside
your own mother's newborn body, itself made
from the stuff your grandmother carried within hers
when at twelve she packed her belongings
and left the Scottish island she'd known—all
she'd ever known—on a ship bound for Ellis Island,
carrying within her your mother, you, the great
human future that dwells now inside the bodies
of your children, the young, which, like you,
belong to the world.

Donika Kelly

Donika Kelly is the author of *The Renunciations*, winner of the Anisfield-Wolf Book Award in poetry, and *Bestiary*, the winner of the 2015 Cave Canem Poetry Prize, a Hurston/Wright Legacy Award, and a Kate Tufts Discovery Award. A recipient of a fellowship from the National Endowment for the Arts, she is a Cave Canem graduate fellow and founding member of the collective Poets at the End of the World. She currently lives in Iowa City, where she teaches creative writing at the University of Iowa.

WHEN THE FACT OF YOUR GAZE MEANS
NOTHING, THEN YOU ARE TRULY ALONGSIDE

late spring wind sounds an ocean
through new leaves. later the same
wind sounds a tide. later still the dry

sound of applause: leaves chapped
falling, an ending. this is a process.
the ocean leaping out of ocean

should be enough. the wind
pushing the water out of itself;
the water catching the light

should be enough. I think this
on the deck of one boat
then another. I think this

in the Salish, thought it in Stellwagen
in the Pacific. the water leaping
looks animal, looks open mouthed,

looks toothed and rolling;
the ocean an animal full
of other animals.

what I am looking for doesn't matter.
that I am looking doesn't matter.
I exert no meaning.

a juvenile bald eagle eats
a harbor seal's placenta.
its head still brown.

this is a process. the land
jutting out, seals hauled out,
the white-headed eagles lurking

ready to take their turn at what's left.
the lone sea otter on its back,
toes flopped forward and curled;

Friday Harbor: the phone booth
the ghost snare of a gray whale's call;
an orca's tooth in an orca's skull

mounted inside the glass box.
remains. this is a process.
three river otters, two adults, a pup,

roll like logs parallel to the shore.
two doe, three fawns. a young buck
stares, its antlers new, limned gold

in sunset. then the wind again:
a wave through leaves green
with deep summer, the walnut's

green husk. we are alive in a green
crashing world. soon winter.
the boat forgotten. the oceans,

their leaping animal light, off-screen.
past. future. this is a process. the eagles
at the river's edge cluster

in the bare tree. they steal fish
from ducks. they eat the hunter's
discards: offal and lead. the juveniles

practice fighting, their feet tangle
midair before loosing. this
is a process. where they came from.

for how long will they stay.
that I am looking doesn't matter.
I will impose no meaning.

Joy Harjo

Joy Harjo is the 23rd Poet Laureate of the United States, and a
member of the Muscogee Nation; she is also the author of ten books
of poetry, seven music albums, two memoirs, and several plays
and children's books. Her honors include Yale's 2023 Bollingen
Prize for American Poetry, a National Book Critics Circle Ivan
Sandrof Lifetime Achievement Award, a Ruth Lilly Poetry Prize,
a Guggenheim Fellowship, and a Tulsa Artist Fellowship. She is a
chancellor of the Academy of American Poets, the chair of the Native
Arts & Cultures Foundation, and the inaugural Artist-in-Residence
for the Bob Dylan Center in Tulsa, Oklahoma, where she lives.

EAT

Grasshoppers devoured the sunflowers
Petal by petal to raggedy yellow flags—
Squash blossoms of small suns blessed
By dew drops flared beauty in the morning
Until an army of squash bugs landed
And ate, then dragged their bellies
From the carnage—
Field mice chewed their way
Into the house. They eat anything
Sweet and leave their pebbled shit
In staggered lines to the closet door—
Hungry tree frogs clung to the screen
Their curled tongues catch anything
With wings driven to the light—
We found a snake hidden on the porch,
There were rumors in the yard
Of fat mice frolicking here.
The night is swallowing
Daylight.

We sit down to eat.

Kevin Young

Kevin Young is the author of fifteen books of poetry and prose, including *Stones*, shortlisted for the T. S. Eliot Prize; *Blue Laws: Selected & Uncollected Poems 1995–2015*, longlisted for the National Book Award; *Book of Hours*, winner of the Lenore Marshall Prize from the Academy of American Poets; *Jelly Roll: a blues*, a finalist for both the National Book Award and the Los Angeles Times Book Prize for Poetry; and *The Grey Album*, winner of the Graywolf Press Nonfiction Prize and the PEN Open Book Award, a *New York Times* Notable Book, and a finalist for the National Book Critics Circle Award for criticism. A chancellor of the Academy of American Poets and a member of the American Academy of Arts and Sciences, Young is the poetry editor of the *New Yorker*, where he hosts the poetry podcast. He lives and works in Washington, D.C.

SNAPDRAGON

Of late the dead
    have quit
their midnight

visits. They ask
    to swing by
sometime, without

ringing first—
    Thank you, no.
Think I'll stay here,

friends, in sunlight
    at the start
of summer, the snapdragons

& daylilies bright
    my son plucks.

Down the road
    the dandelions bloom
in a garden of stone.

A garland of souls.

Like the vines
    I'll climb—
like children who join

their limbs to the silver
    maple's, waving
to all who pass on by.

Eduardo C. Corral

Eduardo C. Corral is the son of Mexican immigrants. He's the author of *Guillotine*, published by Graywolf Press, and *Slow Lightning*, which won the 2011 Yale Series of Younger Poets competition. He's the recipient of a Guggenheim Fellowship, a Lannan Foundation Literary Fellowship, a Whiting Writers' Award, a National Endowment for the Arts Fellowship, and a Hodder Fellowship from Princeton University. He teaches in the MFA program at North Carolina State University.

TO A BLOSSOMING SAGUARO

You have kin in Mexico.
Shooting you is called "cactus plugging."
Humidity & wind speed shape the path of a bullet.
Your shadow will outlive my father.
That's kind of comforting.
Ghost-faced bats pollinate your dog-eared flowers
which smell like wet rope, melon.
The sky is a century with no windows.
I say things like that. Sorry.
You have more rights than the undocumented:
I need a permit to uproot you.
Ofelia believes only rain can touch all of you.
My mother is my favorite immigrant.
After her? The sonnet.

Diane Seuss

Diane Seuss is the author of six books of poetry. *frank: sonnets* was the winner of a Los Angeles Times Book Prize, as well as the PEN/ Voelcker Award for Poetry, the National Book Critics Circle Award, and the Pulitzer Prize. *Still Life with Two Dead Peacocks and a Girl* was a finalist for the National Book Critics Circle Award and the Los Angeles Times Book Prize. *Four-Legged Girl* was a finalist for the Pulitzer Prize. *Wolf Lake, White Gown Blown Open* received the Juniper Prize. Her sixth collection, *Modern Poetry*, is forthcoming in March 2024. Seuss was the recipient of a Guggenheim Fellowship in 2020, as well as the John Updike Award from the American Academy of Arts and Letters in 2021. She was raised by a single mother in rural Michigan, which she continues to call home.

NATURE, WHICH CANNOT BE DRIVEN TO

To drive to it is to drive through it.
Like a stalker, it is in the back seat of the car.
It's in the passenger seat, and the wires of the radio.
You want to think of it as a destination,

a two-week break from purchase power.
Though you have purchased much to get there.
Certain shoes, with certain soles.
Like an exile in a self-made skiff

in the middle of a tortured sea, nature
is what you have done to it.
Nature is you, and the doing to it,
and your platitudes, and the wishing

you could do more, or could have done more.
Could have done—a part of speech referred to as
a "modal of lost opportunities." Nature
is the parts of speech, having learned them,

and having forgotten them. It is the singular
pronoun "you" looking in the mirror,
realizing you could have done more to hold on
to your beauty. Who are you kidding?

You were never beautiful. There was nothing
to hold on to. Nature is how you were born,
with a birthmark that blazed when you cried
centered right between your brows

like a bullseye. *There was a time,* you want to say.
You fed apples to horses through barbed wire
fences. You slept for nights on end
in a fishing shack built on a pier in the middle

of a pond deeper than anyone could calculate.
You knew where the morels grew,
and the watercress, which you pulled and ate
without embellishment. What did it taste like?

It tasted green. Nature is this sort of nostalgia.
It is human nature. How you parse and equivocate,
your selective memory. The tilt of your sentences.
Without habitat, nature encroaches, stripping

the pods from garden peas in the suburbs.
If you have the guts to walk at 3 a.m. you will see
whole antlered herds under the stars, chewing
and peeing at the same time, and watch

the pee steam in the induction light of street lamps.
Foxes hurry down sidewalks
as if they are late for a meeting, counting
their steps, a number which will legitimize

their presence on the planet. No wonder
their smiles are self-satisfied. Rabbits leap
in patterns across boulevards named after trees.
There is something in suburban rabbits

that has evolved toward wickedness,
their tails like an implement developed
for hospitals, to mop up blood.
Nature cannot be redeemed. It is your wish

to redeem it, to set things right.
It is the impossibility of redemption.
It is the lover walking out, their self-justified gait
as they disappear through the tunnel of flowers.

Victoria Chang

Victoria Chang's most recent collection of poems, *With My Back to the World,* is forthcoming in 2024. Her latest book of poetry is *The Trees Witness Everything.* Her book of nonfiction, *Dear Memory,* was published in 2021. *OBIT,* her prior book of poems, received the Los Angeles Times Book Prize, the Anisfield-Wolf Book Award in Poetry, and the PEN/Voelcker Award. She has received a Guggenheim Fellowship and the Chowdhury International Prize in Literature. She is the Bourne Chair in Poetry at Georgia Tech and current director of Poetry@Tech.

A WOMAN WITH A BIRD

A bald eagle called out to another as magpies attacked
their nest. Someone called it *romantic*. I believed her.

The magpies, the ferryman, God, the poets, everything
seemed romantic in Alaska, where people breathed out

white birds. When I breathed, nothing came out. The
eagles sat side by side and I wondered why they

stayed long after the magpies had gone. At first, I thought
the eagle was watching me. Then I realized the

eagle was my life watching me. The distance between my
life and myself had become too far. Because of my

desire to find a way out of my life. When that happens,
our breath comes out elsewhere. As if each day, I walked

in a door but came out of another door. I wondered what
country my breath came out in. When the male

eagle finally flew off to a distant tree, the female didn't
follow. I felt something in my body attach and heard a

clicking noise. I had been holding my breath for decades,
while others painted my breasts, one white, one brown.

In Alaska, my life was with me again, attached for now. I
took photos of the birds to remind myself that the

unsettled feeling wasn't caused by me, and could be
solved by traveling somewhere cold.

Gabrielle Calvocoressi

Gabrielle Calvocoressi is the author of *The Last Time I Saw Amelia Earhart, Apocalyptic Swing* (a finalist for the Los Angeles Times Book Prize), and *Rocket Fantastic*, winner of the Audre Lorde Award for Lesbian Poetry. Calvocoressi is the recipient of numerous awards and fellowships, including a Stegner Fellowship and Jones Lectureship from Stanford University; a Rona Jaffe Woman Writer's Award; a Lannan Foundation residency in Marfa, Texas; the Bernard F. Conners Prize from the *Paris Review;* and a residency from the Civitella di Ranieri Foundation, among others. Calvocoressi's poems have been published or are forthcoming in numerous magazines and journals including the *New York Times, Poetry*, the *Kenyon Review, Tin House,* and the *New Yorker.* Calvocoressi teaches at UNC Chapel Hill and lives in Old East Durham, North Carolina, where joy, compassion, and social justice are at the center of their personal and poetic practice. Calvocoressi was the Beatrice Shepherd Blane Fellow at the Harvard-Radcliffe Institute for 2022–2023.

AN INN FOR THE COVEN

Witch hazel going wild along the
walkway. And all the spots to sit
and read our spell books. And all
the ways to keep them out. Two
black cats and a beaver who eats
carrots all day. Every room an
upper room even on the ground
floor. And bee boxes in the way
way back. And the sweet man who
comes to keep them. All our loves
are witches too. Or warlocks. All
our children and all our children.
Welcome. Water running in the
brook. Clean enough to drink from
our hands. And seven sources. And
a deep well. All for us and all for
those we bring over. Four swings in
the branches. A library in every
hollow. And birds. So many birds
we stop trying to name them. We'll
just let them be with their own
names. Maybe they'll tell us.
Porches. Tomatoes in the summer
and pumpkins in the fall. And curry
leaves and curry blossoms. Jasmine
in the rooms at night. All loves
protected. All of us playing
cribbage on the lawn.

Khadijah Queen

Khadijah Queen, PhD, is the author of six books of innovative poetry and hybrid prose, including most recently *Anodyne*, winner of the William Carlos Williams Award from the Poetry Society of America. Individual poems and prose appear in the *American Poetry Review, Ploughshares, Harper's Magazine,* the *Poetry Review*, and widely elsewhere. In 2022, she received a Disability Futures Fellowship from United States Artists, and in 2023, she was awarded a six-week Civitella Ranieri Foundation residency Fellowship in Umbertide, Italy. Her book of literary theory and criticism, *Radical Poetics*, is forthcoming in 2025. Born near Detroit, Michigan, she grew up in Los Angeles, California.

TOWER

A black snake plays dead
on the path between
dogwoods and a meadow of wild
Ageratum, pretends to be water-soaked,
a fallen branch. Others lie
strewn about, their bark-flaked corpses no
mirage. *All is well*, say the midges, dragonflies,
moths, ladybugs, even the wind
stirring the leaves says to trust
instinct's music. I walk to unravel
panic's thousand fingers braided through
my insides—false roots. When I see death
I think *lose lose lose*
automatically. The tarot says let go,
change. I haven't read Gospodinov's
The Physics of Sorrow, yet; can only take
Sharpe's *In the Wake* in small doses.
I don't want to drown in ocean math.
I narrow my eyes to the scam, don't
move too fast, switch directions
then pause—turn back to see
what choice the snake makes sans my alarm.
In the forest, grief lives a new life
as devotion. Early August leaves play at color
before surrendering to both
man-made ground and messy slopes
collecting undergrowth. I wonder what's past
resistance to change, on the other side
of fear. If I don't look down, or walk away. Step
over the snake instead, realize
both living and dying require giving up.

José Olivarez

José Olivarez is the son of Mexican immigrants, and the author of two collections of poems, including most recently, *Promises of Gold*. His debut book of poems, *Citizen Illegal*, was a finalist for the PEN/ Jean Stein Book Award and a winner of the 2018 Chicago Review of Books Poetry Prize. It was named a best book of the year in 2018 by the *Adroit Journal*, NPR, and the New York Public Library. In 2019, he was awarded a Ruth Lilly and Dorothy Sargent Rosenberg Poetry Fellowship from the Poetry Foundation. Along with Felicia Rose Chavez and Willie Perdomo, he co-edited the poetry anthology *The BreakBeat Poets Vol. 4: LatiNEXT*. In response to Olivarez's latest collection, critic Luz Magdaleno Flores declared: "White people have Emily Dickinson, Mexicans have José Olivarez." He lives in Jersey City, New Jersey.

YOU MUST BE PRESENT,

i say to myself when the what wheres
all up in the how now—trees! i turn

to the trees for relief & they say *nah!*
don't look at us. you don't even know our names.

you don't even know the difference between
an oak tree & a maple tree. it's true:

my relationship with (love) (nature) (money)
(fill in the blank) is like my relationship to weather—

i only see it when it's pouring on my head.
i'm sorry to the trees i grew up with.

i didn't ask. i never learned. or even wondered (about their names).
(their families) (their longings) i only dreamed of (me)

climbing onto their shoulders. honestly, i was a ladybug
to them—only heavier & more annoying. those trees i grew up with

were generations older than me. they were practiced
at living in a way i will never understand & all i could imagine

was the view from their crown. oak trees. they were oak trees
with their own history of migration. rooted in calumet city

like me. if i asked them for answers, i wouldn't have understood:
sunlight. water. sunlight. water. sunlight. water.

Dorianne Laux

Dorianne Laux is a Pulitzer Prize finalist and the author of twelve collections of poems, including *Only As the Day is Long: New and Selected Poems, Facts About the Moon,* and *The Book of Men.* A textbook, *Finger Exercises for Poets,* and a new book of poems, *Life on Earth,* are both forthcoming in 2024. She is a founding faculty member of Pacific University's low-residency MFA program and a chancellor of the Academy of American Poets. She lives in Richmond, California.

REDWOODS

The first time I entered a forest
I saw the trees, of course, huddled
together in rings, thin veils of mist
between their branches, some dead
but still standing, or fallen thigh bones
on the desiccated floor, but I also saw
the great buttery platters of fungus
climbing like stepping stones
up their shaggy trunks: tzadee, tzadee,
tzadee, each a different size: small
to large or large to small, as if some
rogue architect had been cocky enough
to install them on the stunned trees'
northern sides, leading up to the balcony
of their one ton boughs. I was here
to investigate my place among them,
these giants, 3000 years old, still
here, living in my lifetime. I should
have felt small, a mere human—petty
in my clumsy boots, burrs in my socks,
while these trees held a glossary of stars
in their crowns, their heads up there
in the croissant-shaped clouds,
the wisdom of the ages flowing up
through from root to branchlet—
though rather I felt large
inside my life, the sum of Jung's
archetypes: the self, the shadow,
the anima, the persona of my
personhood fully recognized
and finally accepted, the nugget
of my being, my shadow
of plush light. I felt like I was
climbing up those fungal discs

toward something endless, beyond
my birth and death, into my here-ness
and now-ness, the scent and silence
overwhelming me, seeping back
into my pores. You had to have
been there to know such joy,
fear intermingled, my limbs
tingling: ancient, mute.

b ferguson

b ferguson is a queer Bahamian poet, essayist, educator, and dreamer currently living across the ancestral homelands of the Arawak, Lenape, Haudenosaunee and Anishinaabeg peoples. ferguson is currently working on a book of nonfiction, *The Climate Sirens,* about Hurricane Dorian, the effects of climate change on Small Island Developing States, and how centuries of far-flung injustice—colonization and its capillary inequalities at local and global scales—have come to cause the climate crisis.

PARKSIDE & OCEAN

there is a kind of memory that feels, somehow
suddenly, like a wound, though not always, not until
one wanders back through: the dark, damp alley the only path
toward home—*every place i have loved has forced me to leave.*
and then there is memory as one might always wish:
bejeweled, like sugar on the tongue upon reentry.
what is the name for the scent that whispers *mother,*
the twanged hue of evening that gestures *island,*
limestone, cane, spume? Flatbush, i have sauntered away
from everything that has called me kin now,
as i have before, but in what little time we have left,
let me remember you, let me remember what lay beneath
your weather—your snow-born streams, your troubled foliage.
guinep, worship, convenience, heel and toe. old dream,
will either of us return to what we once were? to when?

Brandy Nālani McDougall, Dana Naone Hall, Noʻu Revilla

Brandy Nālani McDougall (Kanaka ʻŌiwi), from the ahupuaʻa of Aʻapueo, Maui, is the author of two poetry collections, *The Salt-Wind, Ka Makani Paʻakai* and *Āina Hānau, Birth Land*, and a critical monograph, *Finding Meaning: Kaona and Contemporary Hawaiian Literature*. She is a professor of American Studies specializing in Indigenous Studies at the University of Hawaiʻi at Mānoa and the Hawaiʻi Poet Laureate for 2023–2025. She lives with her ʻohana in Kalaepōhaku in the ahupuaʻa of Waikīkī on Oʻahu.

Dana Naone Hall grew up in Kaneohe, on the island of Oʻahu. Her political activism, influenced by her love of poetry, resulted in the selection of essays, letters, talks, testimonies, and poems, representing more than three decades of work, gathered together under the title *Life of the Land: Articulations of a Native Writer*. This book was given an American Book Award by the Before Columbus Foundation. She lives with her family tucked in a windward landscape on the island of Maui.

Noʻu Revilla is an ʻŌiwi (Hawaiian) poet and educator. Born and raised on the island of Maui, she prioritizes aloha, gratitude, and collaboration in her practice. Her debut book *Ask the Brindled* won the 2021 National Poetry Series and 2023 Balcones Prize. She currently teaches creative writing at the University of Hawaiʻi at Mānoa.

AIA I HEA KA WAI O LAHAINA?
No ka Malu ʻUlu ʻo Lele

1.

He ui. He nīnau.
E ui aku ana au iā ʻoe:
Aia i hea ka wai o Lahaina?
> Where high bent forests in fog?
> Where cloud cover? Where rain?
> Where full stream flow freed?

Aia i hea ka wai o Lahaina?
> Not in the dry kahawai where
> the waters should run to flow
> over all the roads that were
> blocked and detoured to Pō.

Aia i hea ka wai o Lahaina?
> Not above where dark clouds
> should be black with wai, and
> emptying to white until white
> means empty, waiting to be filled.

Aia i hea ka wai o Lahaina?
> Some remains in the thin veins of Kanahā,
>> Kahoma, Hālona, and Kāuaʻula.
Barely in the warm breath of Kilihau, Pōhakea, or ʻImihau,
> in the dry wheezes of Hulialopali, Waiuli, or Wehelaunu.
> Some in nā ua Kilihau me Kapāʻūpili if they come.
> No longer in Mokuhinia.
> No longer a lei for Mokuʻula.

> Drought is an old war.

2.

Aia i hea ka wai o Lahaina?

Wind ruffles   the surface of the ocean

the tide is low   the bare reef exposed

in the distance how sharp

the peaks of the western mountains

as Lele and Laha 'āina became Lā hainā.

                    They planned our thirst for centuries.

3.

Eō e nā kupa o Lahaina:
                    we uē with you,
                    aloha with you.

Kaumaha claws inside us
for the dead forced to bury themselves,

for the missing, for the swaths of black
and benzene that bled into the wai,

for everyone bleeding ash.
We uē for generations.

         And look you, our Lahaina 'ohana: still here

Watch us light propane stoves and cook
venison on hibachi, clean and share fish

from our lawai'a, kalo from our mahi'ai,
everything sweet and green from māla,
from kumulā'au still standing elsewhere,
thousands of scoops of rice—

                         watch us feed each other.
Watch us make our own supply routes
from flatbed trucks, jet skis, and boats
for cots, diva cups, tents, tarps, gas cans,
headlamps, walkie talkies, blankets,
diapers, and generators

                         and bottles and jugs and barrels of wai
Watch our medics practice consent.
Slow and mahalo. Watch our constellation
of Venmo's and GoFundMe's shine.
Watch every kupuna, every keiki
treasured, every 'ohana taken in long after
the expired hotel and airbnb vouchers.

                         Watch us protect the water.
                              Watch us make our own pu'uhonua.
                         Watch us teach them how.

4.

Aia i hea ka wai o Lahaina?

             as we pule, uē, and rage, pule, uē, and rage,
             wai flows and weaves memory and dream—
             our wai maka feed the soil

                         and sing the rains of Maui awake.

We are not cornered animals.

             We will grieve.
             We will grieve.
             We will grieve.

39

And piʻi ka huhū.

And we will still be gentle with each other.

The Maʻaʻa breeze is steady.
We will teach them how again and again.

We can't say enough to speak back
                    the nahele
                          of Kula,
                                the noe,
                              the ao hiwahiwa,
                                the puna
                                to gently
                                      draw
                                          wai
                                              down
                                          these
                                              grassy
                                                  slopes.
We can't speak back
                    the loʻi kalo,
                      the ʻulu,
                        the ʻuala,
                          the kumulāʻau,
                                the lives,
                                    lands,
                                        and
                                            waters
                                                lost.
But we can keep asking:
                    Aia i hea ka wai o Lahaina?
                    Aia i hea ka wai o Kula?
                    Aia i hea ka wai o Maui?

Aia i hea ka wai o ka pae ʻāina o Hawaiʻi?

We can tell our keiki
we protect each other
and all we aloha, tell them
we stayed so we can

                    bring the water back.
We can billow steam
          until it rises so thick
     its malu, its kilihune, cools and cleans

               all of this

                    ʻāina aloha—

               until the wai,

               until the wai,

               until the wai.

                    And hū ke ola.

5.

Lahaina, he ʻāina momona.
Lahaina, he ʻāina i aloha nui ʻia.
E ola Lahaina. E ola i ka wai.

Ashley M. Jones

Ashley M. Jones is the Poet Laureate of Alabama. She is the author of three award-winning poetry collections, including most recently *Reparations Now!* She is the co-editor of *What Things Cost: An Anthology for the People.* Her work has been featured by CNN, BBC, Good Morning America, ABC News, and the *New York Times.* She is the associate director of the University Honors Program at The University of Alabama at Birmingham, and she teaches in the low-residency MFA Program at Converse University.

LULLABY FOR THE GRIEVING
at the Sipsey River

make small steps.
in this wild place
there are signs of life
everywhere.
sharp spaces, too:
the slip of a rain-glazed rock
against my searching feet.
small steps, like prayers—
each one a hope exhaled
into the trees. please,
let me enter. please, let me
leave whole.
there are, too, the tiny sounds
of faraway birds. the safety
in their promise of song.
the puddle forming, finally,
after summer rain.
the golden butterfly
against the cave-dark.
maybe there are angels here, too—
what else can i call the crown of light
atop the leaves?
what else can i call
my footsteps forward,
small, small, sure?

Ilya Kaminsky

Ilya Kaminsky is the author of *Dancing In Odessa* and *Deaf Republic*. He is also the translator and editor of many other books, including *Dark Elderberry Branch: Poems of Marina Tsvetaeva*, and *Ecco Anthology of International Poetry*. He was a finalist for The National Book Award and won the Los Angeles Times Book Prize, the Anisfield-Wolf Book Award, the National Jewish Book Award, a Guggenheim Fellowship, and a Whiting Award, among others. He teaches at Princeton University and lives in New Jersey.

LETTERS

Rain has eaten 1/4 of me

yet I believe
against all evidence

these raindrops
are my letters of recommendation

here is a man worth falling on.

Carl Phillips

Carl Phillips is the author of sixteen books of poetry, most recently *Then the War: And Selected Poems, 2007–2020*, which won the 2023 Pulitzer Prize. Phillips has also written three books of prose, most recently *My Trade Is Mystery: Seven Meditations from a Life in Writing*. After more than thirty years of teaching at Washington University in St. Louis, he lives on Cape Cod, Massachusetts.

WE LOVE IN THE ONLY WAYS WE CAN

What's the point, now,
of crying, when you've cried
already, he said, as if he'd
never thought, or been told—
and perhaps he hadn't—
Write down something
that doesn't have to matter,
that still matters,
to you. Though I didn't
know it then, those indeed
were the days. Random
corners, around one of which,
on that particular day,
a colony of bees, bound
by instinct, swarmed low
to the ground, so as
not to abandon the wounded
queen, trying to rise,
not rising, from the strip of
dirt where nothing had
ever thrived, really, except
in clumps the grass here
and there that we used to call
cowboy grass, I guess for its
toughness: stubborn,
almost, steadfast, though that's
a word I learned early, each
time the hard way, not to use
too easily.

Brenda Hillman

Brenda Hillman is the award-winning author of eleven books from Wesleyan University Press, the most recent of which is *In a Few Minutes Before Later*. Editor and co-translator of more than twenty volumes of poetry and prose, Hillman is a former chancellor at the Academy of American Poets and professor emerita at Saint Mary's College of California. She directs the Poetry Program at Community of Writers and lives in the San Francisco Bay Area with her husband Robert Hass.

UNENDANGERED MOTHS OF THE
MID-TWENTIETH CENTURY

Beige powdery *Tineola bisselliella* with lots of
twin consonants & crowded cratery wings
beats against faux-straw lampshades ˇˇ
& bronze bookends
that prop up the classics only two people read.
Puh puh, go the tile-wings, spelling words into air.
The moth has no Wednesdays.   Nearby, the child reads
in her resister body under a blanket
ofˇˇ crocheted zig-zags.
She can almost read cursive now; there are
curves without words.
Nearby, her mother lemon-oils
the table, though there will be no lemon oil
on albums with yellow cellophane
stuck to white brides
with pert hurt hair. ˇˇ
Puh puh, puh go the little moths,
addicted to secrecy.   Algorithms
have just been invented.
There are thoughts without thinking.
Outside, phone numbers with recently-added hyphens
tumble through suburban air.
Inside, the mother thinks not everything needs to be
worried about—or, the child would like
the mother to think that.
The moth-mothers think nothing.
ˇˇ ˇˇ The moth-babies flutter from sweater drawers
& are snagged like the yearning in dreams.
Outside, new freeways
cross the land: light & form, form & light, extra
space in the ampersand—

Laura Da'

Laura Da' is the author of the collection of poems *Instruments of the True Measure*, which won the Washington State Book Award. Her first book, *Tributaries*, won the 2016 American Book Award. Da' is Eastern Shawnee and a lifetime resident of the Pacific Northwest. A poet and teacher, she has studied creative writing at the University of Washington and The Institute of American Indian Arts. She is the current Poet Laureate of Redmond, Washington, and poet planner for King County, Washington.

BAD WOLF

I husk the houses from the land, each one
as similar in size and shape as the battered
crates behind the shipping store. The lake
wasn't here with its jagged edges and dikes

puffing like keloid scars, so I drink it.
I uninvite to receive more clearly what
the fringed prairie might have been
with its controlled burns and bone games

and berries. In language class, I am learning
the story of the wolf who is perpetually punished
for his bullyish pride—made to pursue a hornet nest
and drown in his own reflection, snout

gleaming with the honey he was hoping to bite.
I repeat phrases and parse pauses from stresses.
The markers I seek are nearly impossible to find.
What is under this water and what was once water?

Here where a trail once crossed, people gathered
then the hop farmers dug axe-heads and projectile
points, *still bearing the scar from the plow.* Within
five miles the battles of the first treaty wars

are under barns and soccer goals and signs
allowing recreational drone flying. At the prairie,
a solitary Douglas fir's high branches start
well above my head, telling me it was once

one of many. I must move the tendons of my chin
and hold my tongue differently to string together
the consonants of my language. To say wolf, I have to
open my lips in a pantomime of alarm.

Molly McCully Brown

Molly McCully Brown is the author of the poetry collection *The Virginia State Colony for Epileptics and Feebleminded* and the essay collection *Places I've Taken My Body*. With Susannah Nevison, she is also the co-author of the poetry collection *In the Field Between Us*. The recipient of a United States Artists Fellowship, a Civitella Ranieri Foundation Fellowship, and the 2018–2019 Amy Lowell Poetry Traveling Scholarship, she directs the Creative Writing Program at the University of Wyoming.

RABBITBRUSH

I've never seen the winter
at eight thousand feet:

long stands of lodgepole pines
washed white, miles of cliff face

snowcapped and sheer
and silvered with lichen,

slow herds of mule deer
hugging the fencelines

wind-whipped and sure
where they're heading.

*Do the aspens turn yellow before
they go bare?* There's a stand

on the road where I've
bought a small house,

a red painted door,
some land.

What hubris, to strike out
for somewhere cold enough

to kill you knowing nothing
at all. Not even the name

of the undergrowth thatching
the slope. A neighbor says

rabbitbrush, and I should be afraid
to be so unprepared: herdless

human, without instinct
for the West. But what

comes first is wonder
at the word, at having woken

someplace new. I once believed
I wouldn't see another winter.

Ellen Bass

Ellen Bass's most recent collection of poems, *Indigo*, was published in 2020. Her other collections include *Like a Beggar, The Human Line,* and *Mules of Love*. In 1973, she co-edited the first major anthology of women's poetry, *No More Masks!* Her nonfiction books include *The Courage to Heal: A Guide for Women Survivors of Child Sexual Abuse* and *Free Your Mind: The Book for Gay, Lesbian, and Bisexual Youth*. Among her awards are fellowships from the Guggenheim Foundation, The National Endowment for the Arts, and the California Arts Council, as well as a Lambda Literary Award for Poetry, and four Pushcart Prizes. A chancellor emerita of the Academy of American Poets, Bass founded poetry workshops at Salinas Valley State Prison as well as in the jails in Santa Cruz, California, and teaches in the MFA writing program at Pacific University.

LIGHTHOUSE

It's late and I'm pushing the baby in the stroller
through Lighthouse Field.
The grasses give off the damp straw smell of darkness coming on.
Walk, the baby commands.
So I unbuckle the strap and set her down.
It's February first and the ground's still swollen
from the atmospheric rivers that flooded California.
We were up till four in the morning,
with sump pumps and sand bags, schlepping
every sopping towel and blanket and bathrobe,
while the baby slept in her crib.
There are no cars here in the field
so she can have a little sovereignty,
as she wanders behind me. And faintly,
I hear her singing to herself,
Twinkle Twinkle.
The whole song. *Like diamond sky.*
She's almost two. I'm seventy-five.
I won't be here when the worst
of what's coming comes. I think about it
and then I try not to think about it.
And then I try to think
because if we don't—but I can hardly grasp it.
I mean *her* in it. The tiny glint of her voice.
Something starts to collapse.
Love and dread are brethren
said a mystic woman in the Middle Ages.
For a moment the sun
reclines on the bare branches of the maples.
They're rinsed with gold.
And then the light is gone. The tree is itself again.
It's time to return the baby to her father.
The long beam of the lighthouse strobes the path.
I put her in the stroller and start walking fast.

Traci Brimhall

Traci Brimhall is the author of *Love Prodigal*, forthcoming from
Copper Canyon Press in 2024. She is also the author of four other
collections of poetry: *Come the Slumberless to the Land of Nod*; *Saudade*;
Our Lady of the Ruins, selected by Carolyn Forché for the 2011
Barnard Women Poets Prize; and *Rookery*, selected by Michelle
Boisseau for the 2009 Crab Orchard Series in Poetry First Book
Award and finalist for the ForeWord Book of the Year Award. Her
work has appeared in the *New Yorker, Poetry, New England Review,
Ploughshares, The Nation*, the *New Republic*, and the *New York Times
Magazine*. In the summer of 2023, she was an Artist-in-Residence
at Bighorn Canyon. She serves as the Poet Laureate for the state
of Kansas (2023–2026) and works as a professor at Kansas State
University, where she directs the creative writing program and holds
the Donnelly Faculty Award in English.

MOUTH OF THE CANYON

And still everywhere the little lives—
stars of flowers brightening the moss,
ants pilgriming the road, an orange
and brown butterfly—such a common
fritillary avoiding the wind in the yucca.

I love the big beauties too—the dark
rain veil making a bride of the mountain.
The old grasses, prescribed fire.
And the ridge where the wind tries
to get under my shirt. The dizziness

of height and breeze and vultures
wheeling, songless and full of grace.
What do you mean the wind is not alive?
Look at the way it courts the shy juniper.
Can't you see its reliable visits every

afternoon? Its secure attachment style
to its own wet and thunderous passions?
Let's go be alive like that, like rattlesnakes
making a cursive communion on the road
at night. They say it's the heat trapped

in the asphalt that draws them but I know
it's the way the stars ambush their loneliness
with their communities of fire, the waning
moon glowing like a hypothesis, the snakes
curling their bodies into a yes.

Jericho Brown

Jericho Brown is author of *The Tradition*, for which he won the Pulitzer Prize. Brown's first book, *Please*, won the American Book Award. His second book, *The New Testament*, won the Anisfield-Wolf Book Award. His poems have appeared in *Buzzfeed*, the *New Republic*, the *New York Times*, the *New Yorker*, the *Paris Review*, *TIME Magazine*, and several volumes of *The Best American Poetry*. He is the Charles Howard Candler Professor of English and Creative Writing at Emory University.

AERIAL VIEW

People who romanticize an Africa
They've never seen
Like to identify themselves
With lions. It's all roar and hunt,
Quick fucks and blond manes.
People love the word *pride*.
Haven't you seen the parades?
Everybody adores a lion
But me. I want to be a giraffe.
I'm already tall and long-necked.
In the real Sahara, a giraffe beats
A lion's ass every day
On Instagram. I've seen
A giraffe shake the leaping cat
Off its back and toss it like litter.
I've seen a giraffe stomp hooves
Down hard on the lion's face
Before it got the chance
To meow. I want to be a giraffe
And eat greens of every variety
Straight out the tree. I already
Like to get high. Lions need
Animals like us. We need no prey.
I already won't chase anybody
For my food. But maybe
I can still be romantic. Maybe
I can still be romantic in spite
Of my pride. Someone will notice.
Up the sky, Not down the street.
You can watch me while I watch you
And the rest of the savanna
From my aerial view. Lord,
Let me get higher. Just one of me
Is a parade.

Michael Kleber-Diggs

Michael Kleber-Diggs is the author of the debut poetry collection *Worldly Things,* which won the Max Ritvo Poetry Prize, the Hefner Heitz Kansas Book Award, and the Balcones Prize for Poetry, and was a finalist for the Minnesota Book Award. His essay, "There Was a Tremendous Softness," appears in *A Darker Wilderness: Black Nature Writing from Soil to Stars,* and he is currently working on a memoir about his complicated history with lap swimming called *My Weight in Water.* He is a 2023–2025 Jerome Hill Artist Fellow in Literature, and he teaches creative writing through the Minnesota Prison Writing Workshop as well as in the low-residency MFA program at Augsburg University, and at the Saint Paul Conservatory for Performing Artists. Michael lives near a large regional park in Saint Paul, Minnesota, where he walks almost every day with his goldendoodles, Ziggy and Jasper.

CANINE SUPERPOWERS
Como Park, Woodland Outdoor Classroom—for Ziggy and Jasper

We stroll the grounds and stop at every tree,
at every chicken bone, each new coneflower.
Their noses lead to everything we see.

I'd be asleep if it were up to me.
Still slick with dew, this city park seems ours
as we stroll the grounds and stop at every tree.

Perils persist—real possibilities.
I scan the grass for things they can't devour;
their noses notice things that might harm me.

Sometimes we'll spot a fox, surprise a bee,
find trash, broken glass, have a sad encounter
on our daily rounds to check on every tree.

Three times we've come upon wild coyotes,
sensed before seen through canine superpowers.
All of them have smelled what I'm soon to see.

They stare. We stare. There's no anxiety.
Milliseconds transform into hours.
We stroll the grounds and stop at every tree.
Their noses lead to everything I see.

Monica Youn

Monica Youn is the author of four poetry collections, most recently
From From, which was published in both the United States and in the
United Kingdom in 2023. She has been awarded the Levinson Prize
from the Poetry Foundation, the William Carlos Williams Award
from the Poetry Society of America, a Guggenheim Fellowship,
a Witter Bynner Fellowship from the Library of Congress, and
a Stegner Fellowship. Her books have been shortlisted for the
National Book Award, the National Book Critics Circle Award
and the Kingsley Tufts Award. A former constitutional lawyer,
she is a member of the curatorial collective The Racial Imaginary
Institute, and is an associate professor of English at the University of
California, Irvine.

FOUR FREEDOMS PARK
Roosevelt Island, New York City

The fourth is freedom from fear . . .
—PRES. FRANKLIN DELANO ROOSEVELT,
ANNUAL MESSAGE TO CONGRESS JANUARY 6, 1941

The weed is the Nemesis of human endeavor . . .
—HENRY MILLER

Then—as if someone had switched on a black light in the sky—

the traceries of dread just visible all around her, the curving
    trajectories of each possible disaster

once seen, now indelible

*

Bristling stems of mugwort sheared to resemble a lawn

rhizomatic: ineradicable

each torn scrap giving rise
to a new plant

hundred
handed

*

The Penitentiary Hospital
The New York City Lunatic Asylum
The Blackwell Island Workhouse
The Smallpox Hospital
The Charity Hospital

"our standing army of paupers, criminals, and sick poor"

This whole repurposed
island

dry sponge of rootstalks, map

of the neural pathways
tunneled out

by fear

*

Her eight-year-old at the beach adorning

his ring of sandcastles with bits of shell and twig reciting the "Day
of Infamy" speech, *"we will not only defend ourselves*

to the uttermost
but will make it very certain

that this form of treachery shall never again endanger us." The crumbling
gray crenellations

*

The smallpox
hospital "our only
landmarked ruin"

"No Trespassing: Structure is unstable" the winsome

insinuations
of bindweed

at its feet
its gaping gneiss face blushed

with Virginia creeper its body a copse of sumac

*

In Korea, smallpox is referred to as "Your Majesty" in an effort to
   appease the god.

Eradicated circa 1980.
Who now will ride

the horses made of straw
made to tempt the smallpox

spirits to ride home?

*

Plaques of cellophane

stillness
subdue the East River

The tram released like a dispensation across the swollen sky *"the line
   of flight*

*is part of the rhizome. These lines
always tie back to one another."*

Garbage circulating underground
soundlessly, a system

of pneumatic tubes

*

The monument's honed granite
perpendiculars

a luxury of specific intention, like all luxuries most

poignant at its defined
edges, subject

to encroachment, exhaustion

riprap
loosestrife, prostrate spurge

Hanif Abdurraqib

Hanif Abdurraqib is a writer from the east side of Columbus, Ohio. He is an acclaimed poet and cultural critic whose work has appeared in the *New York Times*, MTV News, and other outlets. His books include the poetry collections *The Crown Ain't Worth Much* and *A Fortune For Your Disaster,* and the nonfiction books *They Can't Kill Us Until They Kill Us, Go Ahead In the Rain,* and *A Little Devil In America.*

THERE ARE MORE WAYS TO SHOW DEVOTION

than we can ever know in this lifetime
once you traced a finger along the traffic
of webs in the distance stitched along
the top right corner of the window frame troubling

the sun its beams breaking apart at the web's
center a single open eye flicking light along our open hands

the spider builds a new web every day bigger
each time in the left corner and then the right the spider once worked

above us while we slept & then in the morning the spider spun
itself into silent waiting or longing maybe invisible but for its hunger

which is another word for desire if desperation were off
the table & all that remained were two open arms waiting

for an agreeable heart but it is like me to imagine the spider
believes itself a failure what with its dance from corner to corner

its web eclipsing more & more of the woodwork with each passing day
& still nothing to show for it but another night of tearing down

& rebuilding & another morning of light stumbling into a window laughing
at the barren web which is a plea a moan a disaster of a lonely maze

I respect the patience of heartbreak how it waits
through the sweetness through the familiar beauty & then reveals itself

through what doesn't return or never arrives at all & it is only you
& a series of blinking memories the moments you had once & believed

yourself able to touch again I think another word for this is hunger
I make the bed in the mornings now every day
it looks new again like no one has ever been in it

Cedar Sigo

Cedar Sigo was raised on the Suquamish Reservation in the Pacific Northwest and studied at the Jack Kerouac School of Disembodied Poetics at the Naropa Institute. He is the author of eight books and pamphlets of poetry, including *All This Time, Stranger in Town, Expensive Magic*, two editions of *Selected Writings*, and most recently the Bagley Wright Lecture Series book *Guard the Mysteries*. He has taught at the University of Washington, Bard College, Naropa University, and the Institute of American Indian Arts. He lives in Lofall, Washington.

CLOSE-KNIT FLOWER SACK

Seedless golden tears,
ferns bound to flesh at off angles,
busted out rez towns,
hemming us in with a cloak of mosses.
The orchestration needs tufts of black shadow,
incidental notes to weigh it down, the blanket depicts a field and loon.
I said we once formed kingdoms at the foot of a vanishing stone.
What was it I said that they said?
"Vividness is Self-Selecting,"
several points flowing together in stonework.
I only use words like stones because we are far away.
We corrupt a landscape through the planting of foreign flowers.
Borders are so often theorized as division,
wending along with a spot of sunlight,
                    "The bone frame was made for
                    no such shock knit within terror
                    yet the skeleton stood up to it."
                    They are not artifacts but fit to our hand,
                    our daily voice,
                    the short mouth line erased.
                    The marsh revels in its glitter
                    and occasional cranberry.
                    The subject is left purposely unstable,
                    we will not be robbed of continuum.
                    The shells fly out from the dress,
                    on strings, according
                    to demands left in the music.
                    Certain stories are told in full frog regalia,
                    the music is allowed its wet set of wings
                    and room to lie down.
                    Words arranged for prayer
                    are in fact geometric forms
                    or portraits of poets themselves,
                    uncovering the dictates of a graven line.

Orlando, are we even
allowing ourselves the present
moment anymore?
There are still two blankets that sit on either side.
Reimagining can take place at the root of time,
out of all necessity
we convert the elements
as a matter of course.

Carolyn Forché

Carolyn Forché's fifth collection of poems, *In the Lateness of the World*, was a finalist for the Pulitzer Prize. Her memoir, *What You Have Heard Is True*, was a finalist for the National Book Award and winner of the Juan E. Méndez Book Award for Human Rights in Latin America. Her international anthology, *Against Forgetting*, was praised by Nelson Mandela as "itself a blow against tyranny, against prejudice, against injustice." In 1998 in Stockholm, she was awarded the Edita and Ira Morris Hiroshima Foundation Prize for Peace and Culture. She is one of the first poets to receive the Windham-Campbell Prize from the Beinecke Library at Yale University. She is a chancellor of the Academy of American Poets, a member of the American Academy of Arts and Sciences, and a distinguished university professor at Georgetown University.

NIGHT SHIFT IN THE HOME FOR CONVALESCENTS

There is much in this drawer that is no longer in use:
a notebook with ribbon to mark passages
once of some importance, a tortoise-shell comb sadly
made of tortoise shell, a prayerbook bound
in mother-of-pearl. Mother-of-pearl.
And sounds: a blurring of bees in the air
no longer heard in the wild.
Everything at once, she had said. All that you
remember must be written down.
Bed linens sailing the wind, curtains flaring
beyond the windscreens, lilacs soon to lie on the ground.
There was a quickening in the heart whenever I saw him
standing in a field of bloom and hum then suddenly not there.
The field gone. The house. The road now under a newer road.
Trees along it long cut down. No canopy of hope.
And the swamp? Who knows what became of it.
Skunk cabbage and buttercups, cattails,
polliwogs and crayfish with their pulse-train song.
We caught them in jars of pond water.
Not for eating no. To watch them live.
Wash your mother's clothes one last time and put them away—
like wrapping a scoop of snow in tissue paper.

Analicia Sotelo

Analicia Sotelo is the author of *Virgin*, the inaugural winner of the Jake Adam York Prize, selected by Ross Gay for Milkweed Editions, and the chapbook, *Nonstop Godhead*, selected by Rigoberto González for the Poetry Society of America. Her poems have also appeared in the *New Yorker, The Nation,* the *Kenyon Review, Best New Poets,* and elsewhere. Sotelo is a Canto Mundo fellow and the recipient of the DISQUIET International Literary Prize in Poetry. She lives in Houston, Texas.

QUEMADO, TEXAS

My grandfather vanished into the land of the yellow jackets,
swerving in their upper kingdoms. The land of the rattlers,
ensconced in the cool of a wide, flat rock. The dry land,
where the grass is laden with a hungry hue and the mesquites
know their time to burn is coming. My grandfather's outline
is at the welding station. The butterflies, in cream and marigold,
accost the air with a sentient beauty. The boots he wore
harbor spiders in the living room. And his red paisley bandana,
cured with sweat, calls the river line to attention. Today
is a rare day. I have finally had the courage to tell him
what the sky said to me all those years ago. That I am bound
to its bloodline, though I can never know its true body.
That I am, in essence, a peacock. Neither native nor foreign,
just an iridescence doing what nature demands. "What a bunch
of baloney," I hear him say with his signature humor, like a splash
of grenadine, as the sun pours its gold silt throughout the valley.

Cecily Parks

Cecily Parks is the editor of the anthology *The Echoing Green: Poems of Fields, Meadows, and Grasses,* and the author of three poetry collections, including most recently *The Seeds,* which is forthcoming from Alice James Books. Her poems appear in the *New Yorker, A Public Space,* the *New Republic, The Best American Poetry 2022,* and elsewhere. She teaches in the MFA Program at Texas State University and lives in Austin, Texas.

HACKBERRY

A place I love is about to disappear.
When the summer sunset drives
into the west side
of our house, burning
with a heat we've been warned about,

I look out the two square windows
that are filled with hackberry leaves whose greens
vary according to light and wind
and whose shade composes a sort-of room
for us, under the tree.

It's said that those who sleep under a hackberry
will be protected from evil spirits,
and I can't stop thinking of how the four of us for years
blithely slept the sleep of the protected, as if
there were no other sleep, and how

in the daytime, the tree arranged its shade
to let hearts of sunlight fall
on the stone path underneath it. How a scar
on the tree's bark looked like a brown moth
pressed unendingly against it.

For months all I've wanted is the blessing
of an open window. Maybe also
I've wanted to sleep through the night.
Tonight is the last night we'll sleep
under the hackberry whose leaves

at sunset cause the walls
and floor to shimmer—
it reminds me of crying.

You can see the tree from the whole house, June says.
When I was younger and walked barefoot on the sharp stones,
   Calla says, I stepped on its roots because they were
     smooth.

 Kretzschmaria deusta, a beautifully named fungus
    ate the roots from the inside

  and now what held my daughter's weight
are columns of nothing. Now
the tips of the live oaks softly brush
  the tips of the hackberry canopy.
     I would like to believe in tenderness.

  Earlier today, I tried my arms
around the tree
but they wouldn't wrap all the way
  around and, actually, the tree scratched
    my skin, and tomorrow

  a crew will cut it down.
Some people call a hackberry
a junk tree or trash tree,
  throwing shade. I love the tree's shade, and now
    it will be gone,

  as well as the sunlight in the shape
of love, and the evil spirits
will do as they please with our nights.
  How do I write this poem, I ask my family
    as we sit together in the disappearing room.

Danez Smith

Danez Smith is the author of three collections of poems, including *Homie* and *Don't Call Us Dead*. For their work, Smith has won the Forward Prize for Best Collection, the Minnesota Book Award in Poetry, the Lambda Literary Award for Gay Poetry, the Kate Tufts Discovery Award, and has been a finalist for the NAACP Image Award in Poetry, the National Book Critics Circle Award, and the National Book Award. Smith's poetry and prose have been featured in *Vanity Fair*, the *New York Times*, the *New Yorker*, *GQ*, *The Best American Poetry*, and on *The Late Show with Stephen Colbert*. They are a member of the Dark Noise Collective. Former co-host of the Webby-nominated podcast *VS* (*Versus*), they live in Minneapolis, Minnesota, near their people. Their fourth collection of poems, *Bluff*, is forthcoming in August 2024.

TWO DEER IN A SOUTHSIDE CEMETERY

we attend to where the dead begin.
the grasses they rose through in our teeth.
we were here before the people
& here before the people who ate the people,
our mouths older than the hunger after war.
you could not survive our music.
we sing to your dead, who we cannot kill.
our sisters bashed on the roadside,
we trample your missed in their names.
they know us as the drums in their dirt sky.
keep out, we could confuse you for dead.
we might put a song on your head.

//

we are loyal to the moon. we lie to the sun,
but the sun doesn't notice us, you do, in it,
your mind making ghosts of us, you take our pictures
throw us your bread.   fools
we have your dead and have seen what
you do with yours, how you make them.
why have your gods allowed you?
so arrogant   so soft
if we had horns, we'd do your god's work.
we'd lift you in the air.
we'd lay you on the green earth.
our horns red until rain.

//

why do we live in here with the dead?
my daughter ask me, I tell her *because we will live
in here where the men are dead.*
why are they dead? she ask. *because of men,*

I tell her, *and outside, where the men are*
alive, they will make us dead, I remind her
what we know, *we saw the fires in the sky*
we heard the name everywhere like wind
forge void. gorge cloyed. they ate the city.
we love them then. then, nothing. they ate
what killed them, it grew back like grass.
then they forgot their teeth.

//

is this a cage? she ask me at the edge.
it is a cage, I tell her, lifting my mouth
from the grass. *who put us here?* she ask
licking the rust from the black bars.
their world appeared around us
then their dead soon followed
we are older than these limits.
so why are we in the cage?
because we need to survive.
why do we need to be in the cage to survive?
because they will make use of us
if they don't find us beautiful.

//

who is my father? she ask me, I don't have
language for her, for us, the night I fell asleep
at my mother's side and woke with her
cradled toward my milk, only the mouthless moon
could confess, no answer in her light,
my mother, my daughter, my portal, my sum
my maker, my making, my composer, my note
I don't have language for what she wants
and even in language a him can't happen.
the moon won't speak. *who is my mother?*

86

I ask her. She lowers her head to the grass.
she opens her mouth. yes, my girl. that way.

//

this way, I tell her, hearing the sound, but she's headed
already, having heard, and felt, as our green dead
ground feels, but did not hear, having felt instead
the tiny drum, no, being the drum, it felt the hand
he was as he hit the sidewalk, under which
is the ground, the ground felt the thump, the near dead
rattled a welcome as he laid there working on dying
his cooling finger pointed south, the hole in his blue
a river of robins, red wax that don't dry, but will seal
what language failed, the hole in his blue a badge of space
a red hope streaming to the gate, pooling in our grass.
my daughter first, then I, we lower our mouths
to red-black ground. it taste like where
the black gate turns brown. it taste like it opens.

Paul Guest

Paul Guest is the author of four collections of poetry, most recently *Because Everything Is Terrible*, and a memoir, *One More Theory About Happiness.* His writing has appeared in *Poetry,* the *Paris Review, Tin House, Slate, New England Review,* the *Southern Review,* the *Kenyon Review, Ploughshares,* and numerous other publications. A Guggenheim Fellow and Whiting Award winner, he lives in Charlottesville, Virginia.

WALKING THE LAND

Because I was terrified, I learned nothing.
I had stepped in a papery nest of ground wasps:
a hateful swarm of them
wreathed up around me and writhed
and sang wordless rage.
One stung me on the neck
and I think I was shocked
more than I was hurt:
afraid of moving even an inch
because that was what the world had become.
I wonder if its frantic sting
was death for the insect whose mind was all red.
I don't know my mind
so I'm making up a story:
whistling past a graveyard.
Something about a goose,
forever honking and charging, flogging, flying.
My grandfather there
and muscadines in the Georgia heat.
My grandfather smoked Winstons
and what could be more American
than choosing one's future
decline. He broke one apart
in his palm, spat into it,
and smeared the poultice over my angry skin.
Would you call it a wound,
I asked a doctor
because there are hurts
that mean so little.
I want to say nothing imprecise.
I want to stand
(like I could, then)
in the pine shade of those trees

and not fill up
with murky nausea, soothed some by nicotine.
This will help,
my grandfather said. Like magic, you wait and see.

Paisley Rekdal

Paisley Rekdal is the author of four books of nonfiction and seven books of poetry, including *Nightingale*, *Appropriate: A Provocation*, and most recently *West: A Translation*. She is the editor and creator of the digital archive projects West, Mapping Literary Utah, and Mapping Salt Lake City. Her work has received the Amy Lowell Poetry Traveling Fellowship, a Guggenheim Fellowship, an NEA Fellowship, Pushcart Prizes, the Academy of American Poets Laureate Fellowship, a Fulbright Fellowship, and various state arts council awards. The former Utah Poet Laureate, she teaches at the University of Utah where she is a distinguished professor.

TAKING THE MAGNOLIA

Always, I'd said, of this slow
    upswelling: flames
of white, purple—Royal

    Purple they called
this magnolia—
    the winds shivered, split

to its drought-splintered
    crotch. The tree
will not make it

    a fifteenth, a twentieth
winter. I watched it,
    once, eased

into the ground where
    a neighbor planted it;
now I watch her son

    take it down, take with it
all the buds of its
    renewing, flowers

always on the verge
    of flowering
into a future

    that will not
reliably come. *Always*
    is not a word

we are allowed
    to use anymore
about anything

in the world. We must
put some part of it
    into a category

of pure mind now: no
    deepening snow, no
blue-eyed glacier, the damp-

    skinned buds peeled open
only to rot.
    A thousand candles,

thousand mouths
    widen their pinks
atop what the arborist calls

    unhealable wound.
I need to slip
    this tree inside

myself: crystallize
    its images
into words which,

    if never
made real, are still
    reproducible.

What purpose, otherwise,
    is grief?
Otherwise

    why watch this tree
wither to ground,
    why follow it to its final

abandonment? Here
    is my small
replenishing: each year

    making the flowers
in mind more
    vibrant, plentiful.

It feeds
    some kind of denial, yes,
but without which

    no past, no
future left
    to choose from.

The tree inside me
    grows. I hold
its thousand tongues, thousand fires

    alight. They will
never burn you, no—
    though no one

will ever put them out.

Matthew Zapruder

Matthew Zapruder is the author of five collections of poetry, most recently *Story of a Poem, Father's Day,* and *Why Poetry*. He is editor-at-large at Wave Books, where he edits contemporary poetry, prose, and translations. From 2016–2017, he held the annually rotating position of editor of the Poem column for the *New York Times Magazine*, and was the editor of the anthology *The Best American Poetry 2022*. He teaches in the MFA in Creative Writing program at Saint Mary's College of California, and lives in the Bay Area of Northern California.

IT WAS SUMMER. THE WIND BLEW

It was summer. The wind blew
away from me, and I stayed here thinking
about a certain mountain. Things got green
then forgot, and in their forgetting
remembered everything that was not
grass, or me. My son forgot
he could not swim, then emerged
tall as laughter, hidden
as the lesson in a song. He forgot
how to tie his shoes then
learned how to draw a face
and tie it to a string and run far off
into the place only he could go.
I chased him but he just grew larger.
For a week he became a carpenter,
hammering filled my heart. My heart
went to the hardware store and bought
all the napping spatulas. It was
summer, so I let them stay up
all night, or they let me.
We swung from the magnolia,
our great leaves fell, it remained
our friend. Each day was that same
sweet holiday that never ended
until the windows got soft. It was summer.
Candles came on like televisions.
That was the last time things were real.

Prageeta Sharma

Prageeta Sharma is the author of five poetry collections, most recently *Grief Sequence*, a narrative reflection on grief over the loss of a loved one; *Undergloom*; and *Infamous Landscapes*. She is the founder of the conference Thinking Its Presence: An Interdisciplinary Conference on Race, Creative Writing, and Artistic and Aesthetic Practices. A recipient of the 2010 Howard Foundation Award and a finalist for the Poetry Society of America's 2020 Four Quartets Prize, she has taught at The New School for Social Research, Goddard College, the Iowa Writers' Workshop, and the University of Montana, and is now the Henry G. Lee '37 professor of English at Pomona College.

I AM LEARNING TO FIND THE HORIZONS OF PEACE

During this summer of hospice, my love, where we don't know if we have
days, weeks, or months, we escape just an hour away to Laguna Niguel
whose beaches are a summer salve: an upper limb of the sun dubbing a
    hue
that evades the duress of our current reality. I must try
and see the whole of what's in front of me without squandering it.

I will write it out in colors and hues:
It is the dress of agreeable pastels we haven't begun to wear:
a stripe of salmon in the middle-sky, with rising periwinkle and silver-
    gray.
The sight of a pearling ocean contrasting the rust sunset.
The composition is habitually juxtaposed by drawing its own median
    lines—
descriptions for a worded freedom
in a clarity the horizon affords.

This morning we gaze upon a marine layer hazing
above, dampening our room-air, giving you a worrisome sore
throat that thankfully disappears as we shift through the day.
I am learning that shifting through ailments, in particular,
is how to make peace with anything happening
at any moment, and that moving in and out of tricky comfort zones
is a kind of subtle reckoning with mortality.
Such as your foot stinging with numbness:
you are no longer able to put weight on one foot; or your needing
your nebulizer to open your chest in the middle of the night:
a humming of inhalation to release breath, to help ease pain.

We are learning how scrupulous
details or charted changes or quick problem-solving
invite us to new thinking: through it, I see your eyes alight,

a pure blue sky of mapping after you've been enduring
some pain or challenge.

We work through the panic into insight.

I am learning this again and again.

We know that in Claremont, we sometimes can't see through
anything in our Southern California smog. One must try to lose
all the anxieties in the face of the unknown, I try to think,
and not let it choke in the jostle of lying awake.

Today, I whisper I Love You when I catch your face in a stated
    vacancy,
or when you sit in a reposed silence looking out on the beach from
    our window.

I am writing your obituary on my phone, getting basic facts from
    you.
Where you were born and moved to. I don't know which views you
    had where.
There is first Milwaukee then Tacoma then Silverdale, with its view
    of
the Dyes Inlet to which you wanted to move back.

I know that part of the present moment is that we paid to have this
    hotel view
of the horizon but this will not be as eternal as what I now must
    forge before me:

the will to live without you and frame what you have given me,
that which feels immutable: The windows to expand into who we are
    inside
of our own, of how to make time an unmediated horizon
of catching, fabricated purples, of how to describe the wakefulness of it,
to the fact of acceptance and this holy blush of loss.

100

Roger Reeves

Roger Reeves is the author of *King Me* and *Best Barbarian*, winner of the Griffin Poetry Prize and the Kingsley Tufts Poetry Award. His essays have appeared in *Granta*, the *Yale Review*, and elsewhere. Reeves's *Dark Days: Fugitive Essays* is a crucial book that calls for community, solidarity, and joy, even in—especially in—these dark days. *Vulture* recently called it "stunning" and applauded how it "captures the sorrows inherent in the way we live today even while keeping a keen eye toward opportunity for joy." He is the recipient of a Whiting Award and teaches at the University of Texas at Austin.

BENEATH THE PERSEIDS

Raw cotton on the road appears as the dead
Appear in us, to us, slightly bucking,

Unbidden yet called, not speaking per se
But not not speaking, their scent on our hands

Because we lifted a stone from the blood-
Less river, pressed its exile to our eye. I,

I did not want to begin with the dead,
Their urgent dust and disquisitions, their be's

Being emperor and everywhere, but my hands,
My hands led me into the road, to pull

At the cotton matted to the fresh tar,
Forget the stars wasting themselves across the sky.

I was there for waste, for the Gorgon's head
Held in Perseus's hand, for the sweat

Of stars sliding across his sword, the winged
Stallion bursting forth from the Gorgon's blood.

Blood and corpse fill the sky. Rawest cotton
Gauzes the black wounds of the screaming road. I!

Kazim Ali

Kazim Ali is the author of numerous books of poetry, fiction, essays, translation, and cross-genre work, including most recently *Sukun: New and Selected Poems.* Forthcoming in 2024 are a novel, *Indian Winter,* and a book of criticism, *Black Buffalo Woman: An Introduction to the Poetry and Poetics of Lucille Clifton.* Founder of Nightboat Books, Kazim is currently a professor of Creative Writing and Comparative Literature and Chair of the Department of Literature at the University of California, San Diego.

THE MAN IN 119

takes his tea all alone
—NATALIE MERCHANT

At the hotel pool, a young child is reading, their body language learned
from some adult, one leg tucked underneath them, the other knee on top
They move from chair to chair as the sun moves across the pool
A monarch flutters through as the rain begins its light fall

Why shouldn't the rain signal regret
Not a cold lonely rain of northeastern winter
but the warm California rain, leaves shining in the white air
somehow brighter through the cloud of memory

And I know that I loved him through the swelling storm that
        battered us
Dupont Circle, the birds all calling, his arms around me
We tried to draw our future away from death
I still love him, though lives later and on the other side of the continent

I call into the watery morning my joy of those days
Rope of a flagpole clanking a rhythm
The weather turns, the acacia trunk twisting
How much is possible

As they gather their things to seek shelter, the smiling mother comes
        over
to tell me the child has asked her with wonder "Is that man Indian?
He is so beautiful!" and that the same morning they had told their mother
they wanted to use new pronouns

It's California, the rain always recedes by midday
The day is bright and growing brighter, the child is laughing,
But long years of grief have frozen me cold and lonely
I linger here still with the rain and my regrets—

torrin a. greathouse

torrin a. greathouse is a transgender cripple-punk poet and essayist, and the author of *Wound from the Mouth of a Wound* (winner of the 2022 Kate Tufts Discovery Award), and *DEED*. She received her MFA in Creative Writing from the University of Minnesota. Their work has been featured in *Poetry Magazine*, the *Rumpus*, the *New York Times Magazine*, *Ploughshares*, and the *Kenyon Review*. They have received fellowships from the National Endowment for the Arts, the Effing Foundation for Sex-Positivity, Zoeglossia, the University of Arizona Poetry Center, and the Ragdale Foundation. She teaches at the Rainier Writing Workshop, the low-residency MFA program at Pacific Lutheran University. She lives in Minneapolis, Minnesota.

NO ETHICAL TRANSITION UNDER LATE CAPITALISM
Large hypodermic syringe, peat/vermiculite soil, water, soy plants, 132" x 12" x 12"

Inside the needle's clear chamber, a microbiome. Water and loam and seeds swarming to life. Where it seems as if nothing should grow. The soy sprouts stretch and press against the confines of this artificial sky—their irregular terrarium—roots balled to tiny children's fists. Seeing this, I wonder if the plunger is glued in place to prevent escape. To prevent what little water seeping away. I don't have to check to know the roots are rotting, crept through with mold. Soon, the seedlings will drink this place dry, feast away the nutrients, and starve themselves, unknowing. If I had to hazard a guess, the artist will replace this syringe with another, and then another, when no one's looking. The metaphor is clear, crystalline. Elsewhere, these plants would be harvested and processed. Byproduct stamped with a brand name, peddled by a corporation built on blood and colony. On miles of olive orchards bulldozed, uprooted, razed for monoculture crops. The medicine I swallow every morning. My gender, distilled and sold to me at market price. Each needle, each pill, a seed planted in my body. The roots they grow there, inextricable from theft. From the pooled blood of a stranger. Even if I abandon this medicine that keeps me breathing, the company still makes a killing.

Rigoberto González

Rigoberto González is the author of eighteen books of poetry and prose. He has received fellowships from The Lannan Foundation, The Guggenheim Foundation, the National Endowment for the Arts, the New York Foundation for the Arts, and United States Artists. His other honors include the PEN/Voelcker Award for Poetry, the American Book Award, the Lenore Marshall Prize from the Academy of American Poets, and the Shelley Memorial Prize from the Poetry Society of America. He's a distinguished professor of English and the director of the MFA Program in Creative Writing at Rutgers-Newark.

SUMMER SONGS

The rain, of course, as it dings
every leaf on the eucalyptus—
what was it doing there, on the US-

Mexico border, so far from its native
lands? You might have asked your
grandmother that question, she too

so far from home, she too singing
in her beloved Purépecha tongue—
Mederush cancahuish nirash Inguia.

Again, I'm going to sit and drink.
Drink what? The rain. The sorrow
of thirsting for sounds that take us

back among our kind. Is this why
she sat beneath that tree all day,
sweating in the heat? To water

the soil, to plead to the tulips—
they too displaced—*grow! grow! grow!*
Oh, desperate wish. If they didn't burst

open all spring, not a chance in July.
Then again, who would have guessed
a tree from Australia befriending an

Indígena from the mountains, here
in the arid and dry Sonoran Desert.
Then again, the miracle of summer rain

and your grandmother's song inside
that song. And the tulips aching
to be free, hum hum humming along.

Adam Clay

Adam Clay is the author of five collections of poems: *Circle Back*, *To Make Room for the Sea*, *Stranger*, *A Hotel Lobby at the Edge of the World*, and *The Wash*. His work has appeared in *Boston Review*, *Ploughshares*, the *Cincinnati Review*, *jubilat*, the *Georgia Review*, and elsewhere. A recipient of a Literary Artist Fellowship from the Mississippi Arts Commission, he teaches at the University of Southern Mississippi and edits *Mississippi Review*.

DARKLING I LISTEN

A professor once mentioned as an aside
that there are lines in "Ode to a Nightingale"
written to mimic the bird's call. Maybe
he was right or maybe he wasn't—either way
the class spent a stretch looking, listening,
mouthing the stressed and unstressed
words on the page. On Keats' poem,
a critic writes that "lyric is thus a mode
that simultaneously erases and expresses
selfhood." I think of an eraser and a pencil
working alongside each other. Part of me
can't help but think Keats called
the birdsong "immortal" because
of his poem and not the Romantic idea that nature,
through its cycles and turns, will ebb and flow
forever. Sometimes the ego's optimism
remains beautiful even when it's utterly
and completely flawed. I'd rather think of Keats,
sketching himself back into place. On
the Golden Record that's out of the solar system
now, scientists deemed the sound of birds
important enough to include as a marker
of our planet. Listening this morning to a clip
of what someone or something might hear one day,
I can't help but wonder if they'll
even know what it is. Maybe they'll think
it was the language we spoke to one another
to say what we longed for, the language
we used to say one day when I'm gone,
and you're out among the trees,
please, please remember me.

Camille T. Dungy

Camille T. Dungy is the author of the book-length narrative *Soil: The Story of a Black Mother's Garden;* four collections of poetry, including most recently *Trophic Cascade;* and the essay collection *Guidebook to Relative Strangers.* She edited *Black Nature: Four Centuries of African American Nature Poetry* and co-edited *From the Fishouse: An Anthology of Poems that Sing, Rhyme, Resound, Syncopate, Alliterate, and Just Plain Sound Great.* Dungy is the current poetry editor for *Orion* magazine. Dungy's other honors include the 2021 Academy of American Poets Fellowship, a 2019 Guggenheim Fellowship, an American Book Award, and fellowships from the National Endowment of the Arts in both prose and poetry. She is a university distinguished professor at Colorado State University, in Fort Collins.

REMEMBERING A HONEYMOON HIKE NEAR DRAKES BAY, CALIFORNIA,
WHILE I COOK OUR DINNER AT THE FEET OF COLORADO'S FRONT RANGE

That stretch of coast like the soft spot
    in your self, the heart of your self I call
your soul. That feeling that comes there, when fog settles
    so truly I know I am walking inside
a cloud. Intangible. Tangible. Both
    at once. Sweetheart, I need to tell you something
after we finish, tonight, with this dinner
    I'm preparing—rainbow chard wilted in oil
with shallots and pepitas, herb-rubbed chicken
    already roasting. Even on these hot days,
far from the cool coast of California, when I'm with you,
    I am inside such a cloud. This is how I know
I won't ever believe in heaven if heaven isn't right
    here, with you. Our sunflowers keep coming back,
year after year after year, since that first year
    we drove seeds under our new yard's soft soil.
That, dear heart, is it. It is the softness I need
    to thank you for. I'd be lost without that
part of you that eases up enough to let me in.
    Then closes back around me. For years,
on the edge of California's coast, ship after ship
    after European ship sailed past. An inlet
kept safe inside a cloud. Safe the sweet smell
    of California buckeye and dusty green sage. Safe
the spineflower, checker lily, blue blossom. Unharmed
    the little native bees and yellow-faced bumble bees
who skip from flower to flower. Unharmed
    the coast buckwheat, and the fiery skipper
and gossamer-winged butterflies who need buckwheat
    to survive. Unharmed the lumbering grizzly.
Unharmed, until thinned fog let ships in, the snakes
    and mountain lions too. You've lived long enough,

sweetheart. You've paid attention to your history.

You know what some people will do if let in
to the part of your self you spent so long protecting.

But you showed me this anchorage. Those soft brown
shoulders. The headlands. Here I am. So much in bloom!

And me, with you, in all this soft wild buzzing.

Erika Meitner

Erika Meitner is the author of six books of poems, including *Ideal Cities*, a National Poetry Series winner; *Holy Moly Carry Me*, which won a National Jewish Book Award and was a finalist for the National Book Critics Circle Award; and *Useful Junk*. Meitner's poems have appeared in the *New Yorker*, *Poetry*, the *New York Times*, the *New Republic*, *Orion*, *Virginia Quarterly Review*, and elsewhere. Her other honors include fellowships from MacDowell, Virginia Center for the Creative Arts, The Hermitage Artist Retreat, and Bethany Arts Community. She was the 2015 US-UK Fulbright Distinguished Scholar in Creative Writing at Queen's University Belfast, a 2022 Virginia Commission for the Arts Fellow, and is currently a 2023 Mandel Institute Cultural Leadership Fellow, as well as a professor of English at the University of Wisconsin–Madison.

MANIFESTO OF FRAGILITY / TERRAFORM

In the Grand Tetons on the shores of Jenny Lake
a ranger is giving a talk: *You can gently feel and*
bond with the lichen; she is stroking the side

of a tree trunk. *The little things in our ecosystem,*
she says. And these days our ecosystem is basically
a Yiddish resistance song: "Mir Veln Zey Iberlebn"—

we will outlive them, since there are critically
endangered orcas harassing ships, biting at rudders,
and even sinking yachts off the Iberian coast.

Scientists shun the word 'attack' for these encounters,
claim it's not aggression but most likely the killer whales
playing, finding pleasure, like the female sea otter

in Santa Cruz accosting surfers, committing longboard
larceny. *The otter was shredding, caught a couple of*
nice waves, said a sixteen-year-old dude whose board

was commandeered by the otter at Cowell's Beach.
Multiple attempts have been made to capture her,
none successful. And in the Netherlands, magpies

and crows are turning hostile architecture into homes,
constructing cyberpunk nests from anti-bird spikes—
strips of sharp metal pins meant to keep them from

perching on buildings. *I'm definitely rooting for the birds*
—they're fighting back a bit, said the Dutch biologist
studying the phenomenon. Never mind the record

wildfire season in Canada that made the weather
forecast on my phone—no matter what state I was in—
just "smoke," the unprecedented heat domes across

the US all summer, the ocean in Miami at 100 degrees
sparking coral reef bleaching and a massive die-off.
Before we went out West, every night I walked a path

around Tiedeman's Pond getting dive-bombed by red-
winged blackbirds, which is so common during nesting
season the local paper offers advice: make eye contact,

run for cover, wear a hat or a bike helmet when you
go out on foot. The ranger is still talking about lichen:
they colonize harsh environments, infiltrate and

wedge apart pieces of rock, serve as food in times
of stress for mammals, including humans; birds use
lichen for nest-building. Lichen are possibly the oldest

living things on earth. *We will outlive them. Mir veln
zey iberlebn*—the Jews who made up that resistance
song on the spot were Polish, murdered by the SS

in Lublin in 1939, ordered to sing to their own execution.
They all died against barbed wire but their song lived on.
And in the prairie restoration area, despite the drought,

despite the shrinking footprint of the pond, the ground
is still bursting with a riot of purple and yellow and white:
cup plants, plume thistles, beebalms and bergamots.

Resistance is struggle against impossible circumstance,
refusal, the will to survive in the face of annihilation;
it can also be the surviving remnant enacting revenge.

118

The dictionary offers sample sentences: *they have shown a stubborn resistance to change; government forces were unable to crush the resistance; the troops met heavy*

resistance as they approached the city; he went underground and joined the resistance. In the story about the Jews of Lublin, no one sang until one person began.

Jake Skeets

Jake Skeets is the author of *Eyes Bottle Dark with a Mouthful of Flowers*, winner of The National Poetry Series, American Book Award, Kate Tufts Discovery Award, and Whiting Award. His poetry and prose have appeared widely in journals and magazines such as *Poetry*, the *New York Times Magazine*, and the *Paris Review*. He holds an MFA in Poetry from the Institute of American Indian Arts. His honors include a National Endowment for the Arts Grant for Arts Projects, a Mellon Projecting All Voices Fellowship, and a 2023–2024 Grisham Writer in Residence award at the University of Mississippi. He is from the Navajo Nation and teaches at the University of Oklahoma.

IF FIRE

river brush float on the Rio Grande in very little water
to the north a sleeper fire holdover from last season's wilds
bust sprout
      flame crawl
           the moon mistaken
               for a hole in the sky :
                   if next world
                   still deer soften
                   into field field field
                   meadow hawk
                   rodent nests
                   overgrown undergrowth
                       all tinder is white space
                       its span a mirror
                       your mouth around light

Paul Tran

Paul Tran is the author of the debut poetry collection *All the Flowers Kneeling*. Their work appears in the *New York Times*, the *New Yorker*, *The Best American Poetry*, and elsewhere. Winner of the Discovery/Boston Review Poetry Prize, as well as fellowships from the Poetry Foundation, Stanford University, and The National Endowment for the Arts, Paul is an assistant professor of English and Asian American Studies at the University of Wisconsin–Madison.

TERROIR

Below the willows while they wept, the sun swept its faceless face
down the edge of the river. Ducklings tailed the twilight

light, vanishing quickly, toward the horizon
where, it seemed, even truth and beauty vanished. Below the darkness

darkening, quickly still, the bees mistook for forsythia and tulips
the lips of paper cups trembling, nearly toppling in the evening

wind, half-filled with wine from the cliffs of a country faraway
where the monks, having day after day tasted the soil and the rain, insisted

the grapes contained, in each form, the memory of the land and the hands
that remade them. The monks, without doubt, thought

we took this memory into our form, each body and mind
willfully, though rarely willingly, revised and, night after night, devised

from an idea, the seed of it. We, to that end, could taste and experience
    everything
everything had been and been through. Did you? I've begun to believe

the present, like the shadows on the water, twisting, doesn't have to be a form
the past took. The past has taken so much. Must there be more

to give, to give back, to get on, or away, from this? My memory moored me.
Lifting, now, my cup to yours, my eyes to yours in the light

cast by the dark, I don't know if I can be known like that.
Fresh snow. Clouds of smoke. Flight without wings. Tower. Kings

demanding another story. Another dawn, sleepless, donning another
little death. Hooves of death I couldn't stop for

running through me until I was run through, laid like a feather-
blade, raw and bloodied. Blade made sharp by a throat. From that
    eternity

I found my way here less because and more in spite of, to spite
the land and the hands I'd been dealt. Soil and rain

and wind, blazing and billowing, like the cloak a saint wore
to put out a candle in a cathedral that will burn: my spirit persisted

despite resistance. How could I let the past be fused, perpetually,
    inside me?
Perhaps it's true, and I'm too selfish, wanting all the credit, to savor

the beauty of not having saved myself entirely by myself. Will you
look at that? Our cups are.empty. Here. Let me. Let's see.

Jason Schneiderman

Jason Schneiderman's fifth collection of poems, *Self Portrait of Icarus as a Country on Fire,* is forthcoming in fall 2024. He is the editor of the anthology *Queer: A Reader for Writers* and his poems and essays have appeared in numerous journals and anthologies, including *The Penguin Book of the Sonnet: 500 Years of a Classic Tradition in English,* and three installments of *The Best American Poetry.* His awards include the Emily Dickinson Award from the Poetry Society of America, the Jerome J. Shestack Prize from the *American Poetry Review,* and a Fulbright Fellowship. He is the longtime co-host of the podcast *Painted Bride Quarterly Slush Pile* and has guest-hosted for *The Slowdown.* He is a professor of English at the Borough of Manhattan Community College and teaches in the MFA Program for Writers at Warren Wilson College.

STAIRCASE

I'm not coping very well, but who is, really? I'm somatizing stress,
sleeping badly, eating too much candy, drinking too much alcohol,
forgetting to exercise or hydrate properly, falling behind on everything,
and the sun today is an alarmingly dull shade of orange, a well-cut circle
of marigold construction paper in a pale rust sky. I am looking directly
at the sun because the ash clouds from the wild fires a country away
have settled over this place so thick and so heavy that the brightness
and the yellow have been stripped from the sun's rays before they reach
my eyes, the particulate haze bouncing back the splendor, diffusing it.
The news says that being outside today is the equivalent of smoking
five cigarettes, but I can't stop staring at the egg yolk sun because it feels,
I don't know, important, like I have to bear witness, like seeing it
will make me persuasive on questions of climate change and political action,
or something, so here I am inhaling this carcinogenic cloud of oxidized carbon
when clearly I should go inside and close the windows, drink some water,
meditate, do some yoga, read a book, anything really that is not standing
here staring at the sun, breathing in cancer, letting my mind wander
to the woman next to me on my flight home from Ohio last week,
who kept repeating hoaxes to me as though they were true. I hadn't
spoken to a stranger on a plane in years, and it was nice to feel social,
to enjoy the seatmate serendipity of air travel, and even when she started
recounting lies from the internet, false stories, conspiracy theories,
I thought it would be good practice at keeping my cool, good practice
at being a good pedagogue, and I thought I had been gently and genuinely
persuasive in my debunkings until about an hour into the flight when she said
"You're very well informed" in a way that was oddly insulting, dismissive,
accusatory, as though I was ruining all the fun by actually knowing things,
and I realized in that moment that facts and data would not make me even
remotely convincing, at least not to her, and I should have retreated
to my headphones and eyemask, but I felt committed to the conversation,
and then she started to tell me about God's plan for me, that she could see
his plan in my eyes, and I suddenly wished she had felt less comfortable
with me as she launched into a tirade about how black magic is real,
and how witches are cursing Christians at their gatherings, and obviously

you can't grab someone by the shoulders on an airplane and scream
YOU ARE WHY THE WORLD IS ON FIRE, which is good,
I support that, I should not have done that, but that's where my mind
keeps going, to an alternate reality where I did lose my cool, and I did
call her names, and I did make a scene, and remind me again, *why can't I?*
It is her fault the world is on fire, isn't it? Her and people like her,
people who vote for lies because it's more fun than the truth.
People more excited to burn everything down in righteous rage
and pious anger than to do the hard work of figuring out what's really wrong
and then trying to fix it? Why was I polite when the world is on fire?
If the sun has turned to murky amber wasn't it *my job* to tell her
she's a monster? My brain keeps running so many scenarios, I can't
turn them off, and they're all designed to punish her, to shake her up,
to make her see the truth. My favorite option is the one where I stare
into her eyes, suddenly look shocked and shout "YOU'RE A WITCH!
I SEE THE EVIL IN YOUR EYES YOU DEMON!" before leaning back
and muttering "protect me God from this devil woman" over and over,
just loud enough for her to hear, until we land. The French have a name
for when you think of the thing you should have said: *L'esprit d'escaliar*—
roughly "staircase wit"—named for the moment on the stairs as you leave
the building when you think of the thing you should have said
when you were still inside at the party, but let's get real, just because
someone said something to her that made her go red-pill-looney-tunes
doesn't mean there was something I could have said to restore her grip
on reality. And she's not even here. I know I'm doing both parts.
But I can't stop it. This is my staircase fantasy: that there was some
mic drop moment I could have had, some brilliant zinger that
would have made her worry more about climate change than the imaginary
kitty litter that was never even in a public school bathroom.
My staircase fantasy runs deep: I truly believe that I had known what
to say to change her mind on that one plane flight, I would have known
what to say for the past thirty years, that I could have convinced everyone
I have ever met to do whatever it took to not get here, where the sun
is a faded saffron blot and the world burns every summer,
and the bees are dying, and the glaciers are melting, and the ocean is full
of plastic, and I told you already, I'm not coping very well, standing here

128

constructing narratives of things I should have said to a stranger on a plane
while burning out my retina. At least there's still some pleasure
in a chocolate bar, still some pleasure in mixing a good rye in a good cola,
still some pleasure in turning on the air purifier and watching its informative
air quality indicator go from red to blue to green. Why am I still thinking
about that woman? Do I also prefer outrage to action? Is it as simple
as anger being easier than grief? And oh my God, are you as exhausted
as I am from grieving the planet? Tell me what I'm supposed to say
about the end of the world. Tell me how not to be hysterical every time
I see what's coming. Every time I see what's here. Tell me how to accept
that it didn't have to be this way but that it is. Tell me how to accept this sun,
this fire, this sky, this day. Don't leave me here in these ashes. Tell me
to go inside. Tell me not to stare at the sun. Tell me it's OK to be alone.
Tell me it's OK to be scared. Tell me it's OK to be grief stricken.
Tell me not to give up. Tell me to stop thinking about that woman.
Tell me there are things I can't change. Tell me I have to live.

Kiki Petrosino

Kiki Petrosino is the author of *White Blood: A Lyric of Virginia* and three other collections of poetry. She holds graduate degrees from the University of Chicago and the University of Iowa Writer's Workshop. Her memoir, *Bright*, was released in 2022. She currently directs the Creative Writing Program at the University of Virginia, where she is a professor of poetry. She is the recipient of a DeWitt Wallace/Readers Digest Fellowship and residency from The MacDowell Colony, a Pushcart Prize, a Creative Writing Fellowship from the National Endowment for the Arts, the University of North Texas Rilke Prize, and The Spalding Prize for the Promotion of Peace and Justice in Literature from *Good River Review*, among other honors. She lives in Orange, Virginia.

TO THINK OF ITALY WHILE CLIMBING THE SAUNDERS-MONTICELLO TRAIL
Albemarle, Virginia

*

two Piedmonts nearly
    touch across green water

I watch my hands fill up
    with wilderness

*

these mountains have given us
    so much & we

will not even give ourselves
    to each other

Aimee Nezhukumatathil

Aimee Nezhukumatathil is the author of *Bite By Bite: Nourishments and Jamborees,* and the *New York Times* best-selling collection of nature essays, *World of Wonders: In Praise of Fireflies, Whale Sharks, and Other Astonishments.* She has also written four poetry collections, including *Oceanic.* Her most recent chapbook is *Lace & Pyrite,* a collaboration of epistolary garden poems with the poet Ross Gay. She teaches in the MFA program at the University of Mississippi and lives in Oxford, Mississippi.

HELIOPHILIA

Desire to stay in the sun / love of sunlight

Don't call it an affliction—
call it *affection.* I'd stay under
the sun all day, never hiding
under a copse of trees if I knew

I wouldn't burn, but isn't it
more accurate—that I burn
for the sun? To be pulled to the light
is nothing to be ashamed of: look

at flowers, butterflies, seals lounging
on a rock. Rhubarb sings in dark gardens
but truth be told it sounds more like
a wet cracking and popping. I think

it secretly counts the hours till it can turn
towards the sun again. For me, the sun
has always been easy to love, as easy
as it is to love whatever small light

bees bestow on fallen leaves—easy
to love the light they give just before
they crawl into a honey-hungry sleep,
just before the first fall of snow.

Jennifer L. Knox

Jennifer L. Knox is the author of five books of poems: *Crushing It, Days of Shame & Failure, The Mystery of the Hidden Driveway, Drunk by Noon*, and *A Gringo Like Me*. Known for their dark, imaginative humor, her poems have appeared in publications such as the *New Yorker*, the *American Poetry Review, Granta, McSweeney's*, four times in *The Best American Poetry* series, and the *2022 Pushcart Prize: Best of the Small Presses* anthology. Her nonfiction writing has appeared in the *New York Times* and the *Washington Post*. Knox earned her MFA from New York University. Her honors include three Milwaukee Poetry Slam champion titles and an Iowa Arts Council Fellowship for her crowdsourced poetry project, Iowa Bird of Mouth. Jennifer lives in central Iowa, where she teaches at Iowa State University and in a series of private poetry writing classes online.

CENTRAL IOWA, SCENIC OVERLOOK

At 8 inches tall, 18 inches wide, and 6.5 feet off the floor,
the awning window in the shower's not for light or looking—
it's a utilitarian slit that lets out steam and stops the walls
from swelling their cellularities. September through June,
you have to look up to look out at a sliver of orange garage
roof pinned by late-day hard-water haze that makes it tough
to towel off between the toes, somehow, to skirt the third-
rate third-degree: *Have I ever been happy? How long
has the AC been on HIGH, feeding us our own sour breath
and dead skin flakes?* But by July, garden feelers creeping
up the shower's outside wall get tall enough to crest the sill,
breach the pane, and flood the pale tiles in submarine greens
& squishy pinks from dawn on & on & on. First come sage, sun-

flowers, and bumblebees so pollen-socked they can't lift
off, thus, they lumber over earthstar-perforated patchy grass
like unshaved sheep, dodging the dog, who will eat them,
sharp shreds of sunflower seeds raining from sparrows' over-
stuffed beaks, and swashbuckling chipmunks catching shreds
mid-back-flip and caching them in flower pots. This system?
Insatiable. Seriously. Something (a possum?) dragged a skull
(a possum's?) in through the doggy door and set it in a spot
of empty floor where we'd be sure to see it. Scoured and tan
as smokers' teeth, it hissed, "insatiable." Come August,
such effulgence, it's like showering in a 3-D movie: Gold-

finch squads in Speedos yo-yo through the stems, turn
hard and vanish peripherally. One cad outside the glass
flashed me the shadow running down his ripped finch
abs! I was naked and coughed up a bona fide gasp.

Alberto Ríos

Alberto Ríos, Arizona's inaugural Poet Laureate and a recent chancellor of the Academy of American Poets, is the author of twelve collections of poetry, most recently *Not Go Away Is My Name,* preceded by *A Small Story about the Sky, The Dangerous Shirt,* and *The Theater of Night,* which received the PEN/Beyond Margins Award. Published in the *New Yorker,* the *Paris Review, Ploughshares,* and other journals, he has also written three short story collections; a memoir, *Capirotada,* about growing up on the Mexican border; and a novel, *A Good Map of All Things.* Ríos is also the host of the PBS programs *Art in the 48* and *Books & Co.* University professor of letters, regents' professor, Virginia G. Piper Chair in Creative Writing, and the Katharine C. Turner Chair in English, Ríos has taught at Arizona State University since 1982. In 2017, he was named director of the Virginia G. Piper Center for Creative Writing. He lives in Chandler, Arizona.

TWENTY MINUTES IN THE BACKYARD

The house sparrow flies to the ground
To get the seed that has fallen from the feeder.

In doing so, it flies through a bit of spiderweb
Which works as something like a phone call

To the spider, who then answers with a *hello*,
Careful and very quiet, but nobody is there.

This happens a lot to spiders.
It makes them grumble about the neighbors

Who walk across the spider's curious lawn.
But the complaint is hollow—sometimes

Someone is indeed there, a fly, a moth,
Any number and manner of very small beast.

They try to run away but are tripped up
By the long, thin fingers of the web.

The small thing quivers, asks politely, *please,*
To be let go, followed by a sincere apology.

But a spider does not have ears. This explains
Why it does not hear the house sparrow

Swoop up into the air, high enough
To reach the spider. Few leaves rustle,

While the whole world simply moves forward.
This is the Saturday business of the immense

Backyard conglomerate at work.
If one listens, one might hear

The great, bustling city of it all,
The small sirens and screams,

The caterpillars backing up,
The geckos at their mysterious work.

Patricia Smith

Patricia Smith is the author of *Unshuttered*; *Incendiary Art*, winner of the Kingsley Tufts Award, the Los Angeles Times Book Prize, and the NAACP Image Award, and finalist for the Pulitzer Prize; *Shoulda Been Jimi Savannah*, winner of the Lenore Marshall Prize from the Academy of American Poets; *Blood Dazzler,* a National Book Award finalist; *Africans in America*, a companion volume to the award-winning PBS series; and the children's book *Janna and the Kings*. Her work has also appeared in *The Best American Poetry, The Best American Essays,* and *The Best American Mystery Stories*. Smith is the recipient of the Ruth Lilly Prize for Lifetime Achievement from the Poetry Foundation. She is a professor in the Lewis Center for the Arts at Princeton University, a former distinguished professor for the City University of New York, a chancellor of the Academy of American Poets, and a member of the American Academy of Arts and Sciences. She lives in Mercer County, New Jersey.

TO LITTLE BLACK GIRLS, RISKING FLOWER
A Double Golden Shovel

And then the day came,
when the risk
to remain tight
in a bud
was more painful
than the risk
it took
to blossom.
—ANAIS NIN

Blossom when you're ready, but rough. Be quaint explosive. And
to those who spoke you dim, dismissed your failed green, then
took your witless imagination for manic romps in the drizzle—the
it named Weather was wee drama, cartoonish in the clutch of day.

Risk the lush you have never seen. Forget how winter first came—
the unrhymed shudder, the gray dressed like your father; when,
thanks to the loud religion of wind, you couldn't find your face, and the
painful trick of season moved through you like a knife of ice. Risk

more. Risk smolder. Risk blood flower. Risk voice. (Like you, it too
was often just storm not knowing why.) Risk is why you remain,
bud like an opening hand, sprouting your mere devastation of tight
aroma, why you'll strut thorn, sink flytrap canines into bland satin,

into a landscape of concrete, unloosing the notion of grass. What a
tight-clenched jubilation you are, what a plump thirsting bud,
remaining unswerved in your reach for any sky. If your aim was
to unfurl, terrify, sparkle with damage, you'll do that and more.

Risk lurks in every inch of soil as frost or scorch, and it's painful
the way soil can stunt the upward it insists upon. You're more than

when you were just a whimpering mistake beneath the dirt, the
Camellia clawing for first breath. Risk that breathlessness. Risk

day, risk slap of sun, risk yawning wide, risk the itch and choke of it,
the damned wheel of days, growth and all the dirty water it took.
Then be that quaint explosive. Growl out with howling, red vibrato,
and own everything weather has done to you. Bellow, girl. Blossom.

Ruth Awad

Ruth Awad is a Lebanese American poet, 2021 National Endowment for the Arts Poetry Fellow, and the author of *Outside the Joy* and *Set to Music a Wildfire*, winner of the 2016 Michael Waters Poetry Prize and the 2018 Ohioana Book Award for Poetry. Alongside Rachel Mennies, she is the co-editor of *The Familiar Wild: On Dogs & Poetry*. She is the recipient of a 2020 and 2016 Ohio Arts Council Individual Excellence Award. Her work appears or is forthcoming in *Poetry*, Poem-a-Day, *AGNI*, *The Believer*, the *New Republic*, the *Kenyon Review*, *Pleiades*, the *Missouri Review*, *The Rumpus*, and elsewhere. She lives in Columbus, Ohio.

REASONS TO LIVE

Because if you can survive
the violet night, you can survive

the next, and the fig tree will ache
with sweetness for you in sunlight that arrives

first at your window, quietly pawing
even when you can't stand it,

and you'll heavy the whining floorboards
of the house you filled with animals

as hurt and lost as you, and the bearded irises will form
fully in their roots, their golden manes

swaying with the want of spring—
live, live, live, live!—

one day you'll put your hands in the earth
and understand an afterlife isn't promised,

but the spray of scorpion grass keeps growing,
and the dogs will sing their whole bodies

in praise of you, and the redbuds will lay
down their pink crowns, and the rivers

will set their stones and ribbons
at your door if only

you'll let the world
soften you with its touching.

Index

Acknowledgments

Thanks to the editors of the following publications in which some of these poems appeared:

The Atlantic: "Nature, Which Cannot Be Driven To" by Diane Seuss, "Night Shift in the Home for Convalescents" by Carolyn Forché, "Reasons to Live" by Ruth Awad, and "We Love in the Only Ways We Can" by Carl Phillips

New Yorker: "Aerial View" by Jericho Brown, "Eat" by Joy Harjo, and "You Belong to the World" by Carrie Fountain

ADA LIMÓN is the twenty-fourth US Poet Laureate and the author of *The Hurting Kind*, as well as five other collections of poems. These include *The Carrying*, which won the National Book Critics Circle Award and was named a finalist for the PEN/Jean Stein Book Award, and *Bright Dead Things*, which was named a finalist for the National Book Award, the National Book Critics Circle Award, and the Kingsley Tufts Award. Limón is a recipient of a Guggenheim Fellowship and a MacArthur Fellowship, and her work has appeared in the *New Yorker*, the *New York Times*, and the *American Poetry Review*, among others. Born and raised in California, she now lives in Lexington, Kentucky.

Milkweed Editions, an independent nonprofit literary publisher, gratefully acknowledges sustaining support from our board of directors, the McKnight Foundation, the National Endowment for the Arts, and many generous contributions from foundations, corporations, and thousands of individuals—our readers. This activity is made possible by the voters of Minnesota through a Minnesota State Arts Board Operating Support grant, thanks to a legislative appropriation from the arts and cultural heritage fund.

   MCKNIGHT FOUNDATION

Interior design by Mary Austin Speaker
Typeset in Baskerville

Baskerville is the most well-known of the typefaces designed in
the 18th century by British printer, type designer and papermaker
John Baskerville, who was also known to cut gravestones. The
typeface was used to print an edition of John Milton's *Paradise Lost*
in 1758, the Holy Bible in 1763, and the 1776 translation of
The Works of Virgil into English.